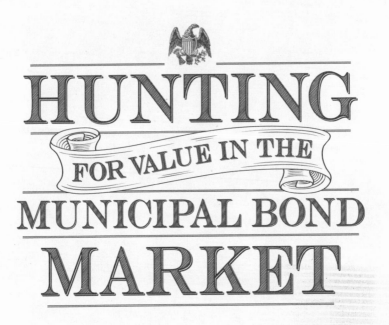

HUNTING FOR VALUE IN THE MUNICIPAL BOND MARKET

JONATHAN R. MORGAN

CRAWFORD
INVESTMENT COUNSEL
Atlanta, Georgia

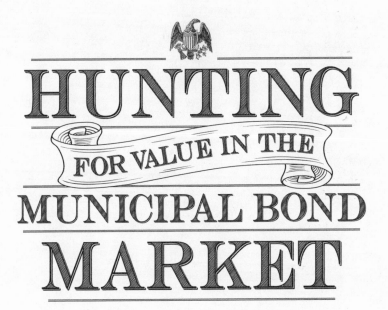

HUNTING

FOR VALUE IN THE

MUNICIPAL BOND

MARKET

Hunting for Value in the Municipal Bond Market

Published by
CRAWFORD INVESTMENT COUNSEL, INC.
600 Galleria Parkway, Suite 1650
Atlanta, GA 30339
770.859-0045
www.crawfordinvestment.com

Copyright © 2014

ISBN: 978-1-563525612
Library of Congress Control Number: 2014956467

Book and jacket design by Burtch Hunter Design

DISCLAIMER

The commentary of actual case studies was written for informational and educational purposes only and should not be construed to constitute personal investment advice or as a solicitation to buy or sell any security or other financial instrument or investing in or exiting out of any investment strategy. The views and opinions expressed herein are those of Crawford Investment Counsel ("Crawford") and are subject to change without notice and there is no guarantee that the case studies and strategies discussed will be profitable or will prove to be profitable, or that the investment recommendations or decisions made in the future will be profitable or will equal the investment performance of the securities discussed herein.

**Past performance is no guarantee of future results
and future returns are not guaranteed.**

Crawford Investment Counsel is a registered investment adviser with its principal place of business in the Atlanta, Georgia. More information about Crawford, including its investment strategies, objectives, and fees can be found in its Form ADV, Part 2, which is available upon request.

FOREWORD

by John H. Crawford III

W
ith interest rates and bond yields at extremely low levels, one might wonder about the timing of a book on municipal bond investing. The answer may lie in history. Think back to 1980 when bond yields were at historically high levels. At that time the Federal Reserve (Fed) had raised its federal funds rate to over twenty percent, long-maturity U.S. Treasury bonds yielded fifteen percent, and high grade municipal bonds could be purchased at a yield of 8%.

Now, some thirty four years later we find ourselves at historically low levels of interest rates and bond yields. While it might be said that it was easy to buy bonds at record interest rate levels, that was not necessarily the case. Interest rates had been pushed up dramatically by investor expectations that rapid rates of inflation would persist. Subsequently, the Fed moved to fight inflation by forcing up short term interest rates to almost unbelievable levels.

At that point, fixed income total returns had been negatively impacted by consistently rising interest rates in previous years. Because they feared that inflation would continue rising into the future, investors were afraid to make commitments in fixed income securities except in the very shortest maturities. Thus, many investors passed on an historic opportunity to lock in double digit gains for the next ten, twenty or thirty years.

Today we again find bond investors in a state of apprehension. In some ways the fear today is the same as thirty four years ago: that interest rates will rise dramatically, and that large losses lie ahead for anyone who invests in anything other than the shortest maturities. It is ironic that the fear of the future has been able to immobilize large numbers of investors, regardless of the difference in historical circumstance.

Jon Morgan has written this book at this time because he believes, as we do at Crawford Investment Counsel, that there are always opportunities to invest successfully in the fixed income markets, regardless of how extreme the situation seems to be. He believes that a well-thought out philosophy of investing can be brought to bear on fixed income investing, and within that philosophy a strategy that incorporates proper tactical approaches can be employed to identify value in the fixed income market, especially in municipal bonds.

While much of what is contained in this book can apply to fixed income investing in general, the book is dedicated to municipal bond investing exclusively. Because of the unique nature of the municipal bond market, investing in this area provides challenges that require specialized approaches in order to add value. These unique features are identified. Understanding the technicalities of some municipal bonds, what Jon calls "bond structure" reveals the challenges of investing in the municipal market, but at the same time reveals the strategies that turn these challenges into investment opportunities. It is always the goal to find ways to identify value in specific bonds, regardless of the circumstances of the overall market.

Even though municipal bond investing has its own set of rules, and the strategies that are discussed in this book are designed to enhance return in the municipal area, there are certain principles that apply to all forms of fixed income investing. Along these lines it is appropriate to briefly place municipal bond investing within the context of a comprehensive view of fixed income investing, and also within the larger context of investing in general.

Whatever the form of investment, the goal is to seek the highest possible total investment return, commensurate with the lowest level of risk. Here we speak in investment terms, without reference to speculation. Balancing these two aspects, highest return and lowest risk, requires compromise, because the goals are inherently in conflict. In order to be successful, one has to be reasonable, to understand what is possible in the realm of investment. All of this relates to the issue of how much weight to put on the goal of preserving capital, and how much weight to put on investment return. It also requires knowing and considering all of one's circumstances, both financial and personal. Each investor has their own way of looking at an investment, what might be called "investment idiosyncrasies." Also, there may be special financial circumstances, and all of these have to be taken into consideration in deciding how to structure a fixed income portfolio, and how best to achieve the balance between risk and reward.

There are many and varied investment approaches that can offer investors the prospect of success. Perhaps one of the more important things to consider in the selection of an investment manager is the investment philosophy that guides the manager as he invests. First of all, the manager must actually have a philosophy, preferably one that has been in place for a long time and has been tested over many different investment cycles. The permanence of a philosophy suggests that in fact the manager believes in it, and that as a result he has faithfully and consistently employed the philosophy. Also, the permanence of the philosophy suggests that in fact the philosophy is well-grounded, and that it works.

At Crawford Investment Counsel we have been guided by a comprehensive investment philosophy since our inception. Perhaps it would be helpful to lift some of the more general aspects of that philosophy, and review them in the light of their application to fixed income investing in general, including municipal bonds. Any serious investor will want to focus on two important themes: quality and income.

Quality

For true investors it is almost axiomatic to focus on high quality in their investment choices. There are many ways to look at quality, but for us it can be reduced to simple terms. We want to invest in entities that give us the clearest view of the future, and thus the highest probability of earning a return. We all know that the future is uncertain, and forecasting what might happen from an investment standpoint is very difficult. In order to diffuse some of the uncertainty and provide a higher level of confidence that our expectations with regard to return will be achieved, we want to invest in entities that offer a high probability of a favorable outcome for our investment. A bond or stock or cash equivalent that offers a clearer vision of the ultimate return is always the preferred investment.

In the case of bonds, the U.S. Treasury securities are considered the highest quality, most liquid investments in the world. In other words, with Treasury securities the investor is assured of a ready market at any time he wishes to buy or sell, and is totally confident that at maturity the principal value will be returned. It is the absolute assurance of these two things that make the Treasury securities the highest quality in the world. Of course, because of their impeccable quality, Treasury securities are always priced with the lowest yield. This makes perfect sense, for the investor must pay a price for the quality of the instrument.

Those who are interested in quality are not restricted to Treasury securities. It is possible to go beyond the safety of Treasuries into corporate and municipal bonds without incurring substantial risk. By investing in bonds that are rated Investment grade and above, higher yields can be obtained without substantially impairing quality, in our opinion. We noted earlier that Treasuries, because of their superior quality, carry the lowest yields. On an absolute basis this is true, but after adjusting for their tax exempt nature, municipal bonds normally provide a yield that is higher than Treasuries of comparable maturity.

Quality and safety, when speaking of bonds, are generally synonymous. With regard to municipal bonds, this is normally one of the safest areas to invest. It is important to keep an eye on the default rate, and we note that defaults rarely occur in the municipal area. Safety can be further enhanced by owning municipal bonds that are backed by a specific revenue source. All in all, municipals appear to be especially attractive for the bond investor who considers the bond portion of his total portfolio to be among the safest and least risky.

Whether it is Treasury, corporate or municipal bonds, the search for quality is of paramount importance. For long-term investors seeking to produce attractive risk-adjusted, after-tax returns, quality is essential. In the end, the lowering of uncertainty of return and the safety of principal is offered most prominently by high quality instruments.

Income

All forms of investment have two forms of return: income and appreciation or depreciation. Bond investors in particular have a great appreciation for the merits of income. This is particularly true in the case of municipal bond investing. While no one objects to capital appreciation in bond investments, it is not the primary goal for most bond investors. Rather, bonds are more crucial in the aspect of income generation.

Earlier we referred to the inability to see the future and the desire to invest in ways that provide greater visibility on future returns. Income plays an important role here, for we assume that the income portion of the return pattern is a permanent feature. That is, if it is a municipal bond that pays interest we want to know for sure that the income from that interest payment will be received without fail. Of course this is true also in the case of other bond investments.

If all investments have the potential for two types of return, income and appreciation or depreciation, bond investors will focus on the income side first. They know for sure that they can earn some income each and every year, but there is no assurance that appreciation can be earned each and every year. And, in those years when appreciation does not occur, in fact bond prices decline, there is the added advantage of moderating the decline in the value of the security because of the positive contribution of the income received. The bottom line is that investments that contain an income portion are safer and less risky. It can be said: the greater the reliance on appreciation, the riskier the investment, the greater the reliance on income, the safer the investment.

Any investment that focuses more on the income side of the equation may be perceived to be a lower return investment. If lower return means a safer investment, it is a choice well made. However, if one is to make an investment in a lower return item, every effort must be made to assure that the income is safe, and capital will be returned upon maturity. As discussed earlier, when considering bond investments, in particular municipal bonds, this should represent the least risky portion of the total portfolio.

Why Bonds Now?

Bond yields are now at or near record lows. In fact, they may be assumed to be "abnormal" and that as soon as the Fed begins to shift its policy into a "normalization" mode, all interest rates will rise. If this is the case, why should anyone purchase bonds today and risk the loss of capital? First, one should not assume that all yields rise in concert. Second, forecasting future interest rates is very difficult, and doing so successfully over short periods of time is fraught with difficulties. Even though we believe interest rates in general will be rising over the next few years, the increases may be gradual. Finally, the third reason is that bonds can always have a role in the overall portfolio, regardless of how high or low bonds yields are. We agree that income is the single most important reason for owning bonds, but there are other reasons as well. Bonds provide diversification, not only in terms of a different type of asset, but also in the pattern of return they offer. For instance, bond returns are negatively correlated with stock returns at times of economic or market stress, thus providing a leveling influence on overall portfolio returns. In other words, when stock returns are negative or declining, almost always bond returns are positive. This negative correlation comes in very handy when stock or other asset category returns are negative. In a recession, for example, when stock returns invariably turn negative, bond returns tend to increase, thus leveling out overall portfolio returns. This is an extremely attractive feature of bonds, and a very good reason for including them in the overall portfolio pattern.

With regard to buying bonds today when yields are low and the fear that interest rates will rise, thus inflicting losses on the owner, we believe there are ways to construct portfolios to counteract this risk. First, there is maturity. Shorter maturities will always decline less in rising interest rate markets, and of course all bond issues can be held to maturity if rates continue to rise. While all bonds are not held to maturity, in many cases they are. If so, risk of capital is eliminated. This harkens back to the issue of income and the practice of looking to the income side of the total investment equation first. Also, as Jon Morgan explains in the book, there are many different ways of creating value in the municipal bond market regardless of interest rate levels.

We at Crawford Investment Counsel are very pleased that Jon

Morgan has written this book. Speaking of Jon, I would be remiss if I did not express my admiration for him and my appreciation for what he does for our firm. He very capably manages our fixed income team, always keeping in mind the ultimate goal: the best interest of our clients. His professionalism is evident in his respect for clients, his desire to bring them the best possible returns without subjecting them to high risk, his patience in waiting for the best opportunities to appear in his markets, and his ability, as evidenced in this book, to explain technical matters in plain and understandable terms. He has been a perfect fit with our firm from a cultural standpoint, and as a member of our management team, a colleague with whom it is a pleasure to work. Thank you, Jon.

We sincerely hope the book is a helpful tool in understanding the intricacies of municipal bond investing. If it serves that purpose alone, its writing will have been well worth the effort. We commend it to your reading.

INTRODUCTION

Jonathan R. Morgan is celebrating his 35th anniversary working in the fixed income markets. His career has spanned historic market events ranging from 20% C.D. rates in the late 70's and early 80's to the Great Recession of 2008-2009. The experience gained by witnessing multiple economic cycles and the resulting effects on municipalities laid the groundwork for developing a trading strategy somewhat unique in the marketplace.

Like many municipal bond investors, Jon believes the asset class can provide favored returns for an investor's safest liquid asset. Jon spent the first 20 years of his career as a municipal bond professional at Bear Stearns and Company. This experience helped him formulate an approach to investing in municipal bonds that concentrates on delivering above average yields without sacrificing quality. As a trader, he developed a deep reservoir of market knowledge that gave him the tools necessary to exploit many of the inefficiencies that exist in the municipal market for the benefit of individual and institutional investors alike. After leaving Bear Stearns, he spent the next decade concentrating on municipal bond portfolio management. He currently is the Managing Director responsible for fixed income investments at Crawford Investment Counsel, Inc., ("Crawford") an Atlanta-based asset manager for whom Jon oversees $1.5 billion in fixed income assets as of the year end 2013. The philosophy is centered on an investment style that considers fixed income as one of a client's safest liquid assets. Capital preservation is paramount in the investment decision process for fixed income, along with the delivery of a consistent income stream. Maximizing income while minimizing market volatility within the confines of a high quality investment approach is the desired result of the strategies outlined.

The fixed income investment team that Jon oversees manages portfolios for over 400 clients of Crawford Investment Counsel. Each client is somewhat unique in their individual circumstances including state of residence, tax status, age, and overall risk profile. The fixed income investment team attempts to put together a strategy to maximize the inefficiencies of the municipal market for the benefit of all the individual clients for which they manage funds. The team hopes to share our insight in to the municipal bond market and hopes you find benefit with this correspondence.

Hunting for Value in the Municipal Bond Market

W ithin the $3.8 trillion municipal bond market there are over 60,000 different issuers that have created over one million different issues of municipal bonds. Compare this to the 8,000 companies that make up the public U.S. equity markets and you can quickly realize the magnitude of this fixed income market. Yet the municipal market is an over-the-counter market with no listed exchanges and only minimal capabilities to trade electronically. Over the past 35 years I have spent countless hours scouring the municipal bond marketplace in a search for value. The unique nature of this market and its large number of issuers create an environment that is fraught with nuances, inconsistencies, and inefficiencies. The municipal bond market is the final frontier in the public markets for an inefficient trading security.

Within the municipal market, inefficiency nearly always leads to higher yields. Therefore, throughout my career of investing in municipals, I have always migrated to certain sectors of the market which tend to trade the most inefficiently in pursuit of higher yields. Conversely, many sectors of the market trade extremely well, with a very tight bid-ask spread. The bonds in this sector are typically referred to as "plain vanilla" bonds. Plain vanilla bonds are general obligation or revenue bonds that are very simplistic in structure in regard to coupon and maturity. A high quality bond with a stated final maturity date and fixed rate coupon will have a large following of potential bidders. This will, in turn, lead to a more efficient trading vehicle versus other more complex structures of municipal bonds.

We will explore in depth the various structures of municipal bonds that may lead to higher investment yields. It is not intended to be a tutorial on municipal bonds for the amateur investor but is more suited for the investor with a degree of experience in the municipal marketplace. The topics explored within this context can be at times somewhat complex. Real world trade data will illustrate the concepts discussed in a case study format. I hope you enjoy the dialogue and gain an appreciation for an asset class that at times can be somewhat opaque. It is our desire to shed light on many of the more complicated sectors of this market in order to deepen the understanding of investors who are seeking to maximize yield while minimizing price volatility within their fixed income portfolios.

CHAPTER 1

Cornerstone of Quality

There are many statistics available that attest to the quality of municipal bonds; they are one of the highest quality liquid investments available to the general investing public. The default rate for the market as a whole is extremely low, and according to a 2012 report from Moody's Investor Service, the default rate for bonds originally issued with an investment grade rating is less than one half of one percent. This places municipal bonds in the highest of quality rankings, ahead of even high quality corporate bonds. In the years since the financial crisis of 2007-2009, there have been municipal bankruptcies. Jefferson County, Alabama; Detroit, Michigan; and Stockton, California grabbed headlines as they filed for protection from creditors. However, even with these large issuer defaults, the market as a whole is still considered extremely safe and of high quality. If even the lay investor uses some common business sense in screening for quality in the municipal market you can potentially avoid the occasional bad apples. Did anyone really not know that Detroit was experiencing financial problems for the past decade?

In my opinion, focusing on high quality is essential to developing a successful investment strategy in fixed income and in municipal bonds in particular. Most investors will articulate they would prefer high quality over low quality for their fixed income allocation. I completely agree. The use of high yield or junk bonds can be a successful strategy for a portfolio allocation, but it probably belongs in the equity risk bucket and not within the fixed income allocation sleeve. All of the bonds in this narrative will be considered high quality. From a ratings perspective, they will typically reside in the AA to AAA rated category of investment. In fact, the investment philosophy I have developed over the years attempts to minimize the credit risk or risk of default of a fixed income portfolio. At Crawford, we prefer to identify above-market yields through the structure side of municipal bonds. In a nutshell, we are attempting to purchase more complicated structures of municipal bonds to exploit the yield advantage they possess. Within the municipal market, nearly all of your total return over time will be derived from the coupon or income side of the equation, so why not utilize this to our advantage by consistently buying municipal bonds that yield more than the market in general. In theory, this should lead to outperformance and superior returns.

Can the average investor rely on ratings alone to navigate the vast municipal bond market? The answer is unfortunately no. In general, I believe the ratings agencies have done a reasonable job within the contexts of the municipal market. Of course they did a very poor job in rating the many vehicles that collapsed in the financial crisis. However, they have been proven to be a decent judge of municipal bond quality. Once again, even the average investor can utilize various filters to avoid most pitfalls from a default perspective beyond just the ratings agencies. Perhaps one should avoid the purchase of hospital or health care related municipals due to the higher default rates they have exhibited over time. It may be advantageous to avoid the more leveraged entities of municipals that typically reside in the public power sector. From a geographic perspective, I think avoiding the more at risk states such as Illinois, Michigan, Nevada, Arizona, and at times California and New York makes sense. Common sense tells me investing in a state such as Texas, which has weathered the financial crisis extremely well, makes more investment sense than investing in Illinois or Michigan. Investors should concentrate instead on economically prosperous geographic regions. The average investor typically has difficulty exhibiting the discipline necessary to avoid the pitfalls of the riskier sectors of the municipal market. This is due to a lack of understanding of the risk and also simple human nature. A higher yield sounds better, right?

Why not pursue higher yields through means other than lower quality or extended maturity? There are many ways to acquire yield in the municipal market without sacrificing quality or extending into longer dated maturities. Sleep well at night knowing your portfolio is maximizing income while minimizing the risk of default. Through case studies of actual trades that have occurred in the market we will attempt to detail various bond transactions to help illustrate the benefits of this strategy.

CHAPTER 2

Municipal Bond Research

H istorically speaking, essential service municipal bonds have been what many believe to be a relatively safe asset class with very low rates of default. Essential service municipal bonds are those issued to finance projects with a high degree of essentiality to the residents living in a particular municipal entity. Financing the construction of a water and sewer project that will bring safe drinking water and process waste is an example of an essential service being provided to a community. Typically, financing for streets, schools, electricity, water, and other basic infrastructure will be in this category and deemed highly essential to the well being of a municipality's residents in order to provide even a minimum standard of living. It makes sense that these types of projects and the bonds issued to finance them would have the potential of being a sound investment. Of course there are always exceptions to the rule, but using a little common sense can go a long way towards avoiding the few bad apples that will always be present. Take for instance the fictional City of Wellness and its desire to provide fresh drinking water to all of its residents. The city has an existing water plant and has a long financial track record. The water system is currently operating on a profitable basis. At the edge of town there is a development of homes built 20 years ago that has to rely on individual wells in order to provide water to each home. The city petitions the residents and asks if they are interested in joining the city water system. The petition is approved and a municipal bond is issued to raise the funds necessary to extend the water pipeline to the development. Residents tap into the line and begin to pay monthly water bills. The revenue generated from the water bills is sufficient to cover the costs of the debt incurred to build the pipeline and to provide a small profit to the water authority. In addition, the revenues of the entire water system will support the financing, and it is not limited to the new homes that were added. Now, let's contrast this to a project contemplated by the fictional City of Speculation. The city is approached by a private developer interested in developing some farmland for a new subdivision. The city approves the subdivision, and the developer issues municipal bonds through a conduit authority from the City of Speculation. Proceeds of the bond issue will be used to build a water line to the new development. The bonds are backed by the water usage revenues received from the potential residents of the new development. Unfortunately, the economy turns south after the water line is built and the development fails. There are few if any residents living in the new development and the water authority defaults on the bonds issued for the project. The point is both cities were going to provide an essential service to the residents but the financing was done entirely differently with vastly different outcomes. Realistically, the City of Wellness would probably have received a bond rating in the investment grade category, while the City of Speculation would have received a very low rating, if at all.

The bond ratings represent a first step for an investor to understand the current financial picture of an issuer for an existing or potential municipal bond transaction. The major rating agencies are Moody's Investor Service, Standard and Poor's, and Fitch Ratings. All three have done a reasonable job in regards to rating municipal bonds, in my opinion. The problem with ratings services as a whole is they tend to look at credit quality in the rear view mirror. First of all, financial statements from most municipalities are done on an annual basis. Therefore, the ratings agencies may be looking at data that is already a year old. Secondly, many smaller issuers may not bring new issues to market very frequently, and therefore will not receive an ongoing ratings review on a timely basis. The agencies will update ratings based on information received through ongoing disclosure requirements, but at times the rating can grow stale. Though it is important to remember the drawbacks from the ratings services, overall they are an excellent first step to understanding the credit quality of a municipal bond issuer. As an investor in bonds, you certainly have the right to ask for a ratings report on any municipal bond you are contemplating for purchase. For the average investor I would recommend a summary report that does not include all the granular details of the transaction. These are typically 1 to 2 pages long and not very difficult to read. They will typically spell out the details of the transaction and how the municipality plans to pay back the debt. Once again, use some common business sense when reading the report. In our case study above, we described two very different financing scenarios. Take a step back, read the report slowly, and try to connect as many of the dots as possible. I believe a logical conclusion can be made from the data given as to whether this is an appropriate investment for your portfolio. On the following page we have included a sample credit report from Standard and Poor's for the Louisville and Jefferson County, Kentucky General Obligation bonds. Take a few minutes to read the report, working through the bullet points, and then the summary text. There may be some unfamiliar terms within the report, but I believe the highlights and overall tone can be understood even by an investor with limited knowledge of municipal finance. "Louisville & Jefferson County Metro Government, Kentucky; Appropriations; General Obligation" originally published on November 6, 2014 by Standard and Poor's Financial Services LLC was reprinted with permission from Standard and Poor's Financial Services LLC, authors Helen Samuelson and Errol R. Arne.

Summary:
Louisville & Jefferson County Metro Government, Kentucky; Appropriations; General Obligation

Credit Profile

US $21.525 mil GO nts ser 2014E due 12/01/2019
Long Term Rating	AA+/Stable	New

US $19.29 mil GO rfdg bnds ser 2014F due 11/01/2026
Long Term Rating	AA+/Stable	New

US $11.33 mil GO bnds ser 2014D due 12/01/2034
Long Term Rating	AA+/Stable	New

Louisville & Jefferson Cnty Metro Govt GO
Long Term Rating	AA+/Stable	Affirmed

Rationale

Standard & Poor's Rating Services has assigned it's 'AA+' long-term rating to Louisville & Jefferson County Metro Government, Ky's series 2014D general obligation (GO) bonds, 2014E GO notes, and 2014F GO refunding bonds. At the same time, we affirmed our long-term ratings on debt previously issued by the metro government. The outlook is stable.

The metro government's full-faith-and-credit and unlimited-tax GO pledge secures the GO bonds and notes. It is our understanding that bond proceeds will fund various capital projects. The notes will fund vehicle and other equipment purchases. The refunding bonds will retire outstanding portions of the 2006A bonds, for interest cost savings.

The long-term rating on the city reflects what we see as the metro government's:

- Strong, broad, and diverse economy given its status as a regional economic center;
- Very strong management with strong financial policies and practices;
- Strong budgetary flexibility with 2013 available reserves at 10% of adjusted general fund expenditures;
- Very strong liquidity providing very strong cash levels to cover both debt service and expenditures;
- Strong budgetary performance with at least balanced general fund operations in 2014 and 2015; and
- Adequate debt and contingent liabilities.

STRONG ECONOMY

We consider Louisville & Jefferson County Metro Government's local economy strong, with per capita market value and projected per capita effective buying income about $86,200 and 96% of the national average, respectively. The metropolitan government, which serves as a regional hub for northern Kentucky and Southern Indiana, encompasses Jefferson County, the largest government in the state. The metro government is home to UPS' WorldPort hub, with over 20,000 employees, a large heath care service sector (with the leading seven providers in the metropolitan area employing nearly 30,000) provides stability. Last year, the county unemployment rate was 8.1% according to the U.S. Bureau of Labor Statistics. Officials note local leading employers are stable, so we do not expect the unemployment rate will rise in the future.

VERY STRONG MANAGEMENT

In our opinion, Louisville & Jefferson County Metro Government's management conditions are very strong with "strong" financial practices under our Financial Management Assessment methodology, indicating practices are, in our opinion, strong, well embedded and likely sustainable. Strengths include strong revenue and expenditure assumptions in the budgeting process, strong oversight in terms of monitoring progress against the budget during the year, and multiyear financial projections as well as a formal long-term capital plan and fund balance policy.

STRONG BUDGETARY FLEXIBILITY

The metro government's budgetary flexibility is strong, in our view, will available reserves at $60.99 million and 10.3% of adjusted operating expenditures in fiscal 2013. For fiscal 2014, the government budgeted a $61 million fund balance, and officials anticipate, based on preliminary results, that they may report a higher fund balance. The 2015 budget includes a $500,000 increase in the fund balance.

VERY STRONG LIQUIDITY

We believe very strong liquidity supports the metro government's finances, with local government available cash to government fund expenditures and cash to debt service at 19% and 2.5x, respectively. Based on past issuance of debt, we believe that the issuer has strong access to capital markets to provide for liquidity needs if necessary.

STRONG BUDGETARY PERFORMANCE

Louisville & Jefferson County Metro Government's budgetary performance is strong, in our opinion, with a surplus of 0.1% for the general fund and a surplus of 1.3% for the local governmental funds in fiscal 2013. Management attributes the favorable result to positive economic trends, but mainly controlling expenses. Occupational taxes comprised 56% of fiscal 2013 general fund revenues, followed by property taxes at 25%. Officials continue to take steps to manage ongoing expenses, and economic trends remain favorable, so we expect strong budgetary performance to continue in 2014 and 2015.

ADEQUATE DEBT AND CONTINGENT LIABILITIES

In our view, the metro government's debt and contingent liabilities profile is adequate. Total governmental fund debt service to total governmental fund expenditures and net direct debt to total governmental funds are 7.6% and 89.4% respectively. We feel the net debt to market value is low and a positive credit factor is 1.5%. The metro government anticipates issuing an estimated $15 million of additional debt in the near term, but we do not expect this amount of debt will have a material effect on debt measures.

We view the issuer's pension/other postemployment benefit (OPEB) obligations as large and, in our opinion, a negative credit factor. The metro government participates in the County Employees Retirement System (CERS), administered by the Board of Trustees of the Kentucky Retirement Systems. In the late 1980's, the metro government closed its police and firefighters plans. The annual pension and OPEB costs accounted for 11% of total government expenditures in fiscal 2013. Last year, the organization contributed 100% of its annual required pension contribution. We do not consider the pension and OPEB liabilities to be a significant budget pressure as officials do not expect overall costs to materially increase over the next two years.

STRONG INSTITUTIONAL FRAMEWORK

We consider Institutional Framework score for Kentucky cities strong.

Outlook

The stable outlook reflects our expectation that Louisville & Jefferson County Metro Government's budgetary performance and flexibility will remain strong, and that liquidity will remain very strong, supported by balances budgets. The metro government's deep and diverse economic base, coupled with a very strong management team that has been managing expenses, further support our view that the organization will maintain its long-term budget stability.

We do not anticipate changing the rating in the two-year horizon, but if economic measures of budgetary flexibility and performance sustainably rises to very strong levels, it could lead to a higher rating. Conversely, we do not anticipate downward rating pressure within the two-year outlook period.

Related Criteria and Research

RELATED CRITERIA
- USPF Criteria: Local Government GO Ratings Methodology and Assumptions, Sept. 12, 2013.

RELATED RESEARCH
- S&P Public Finance Local GO Criteria: How We Adjust Data for Analytic Consistency, Sept. 12, 2013.
- Institutional Framework Overview: Kentucky Local Governments.

Ratings Detail (as of November 6, 2014)		
Louisville & Jefferson Cnty Metro Govt lse		
Long Term Rating	AA/Stable	Affirmed
Louisville & Jefferson Cnty Metro Govt GO		
Unenhanced Rating	AA+(SPUR)/Stable	Affirmed
Louisville Pkg Auth of River City, Kentucky		
Louisville & Jefferson Cnty Metro Govt, Kentucky		
Louisville Pkg Auth of River City (Louisville & Jefferson Cnty Metro Govt)		
Long Term Rating	AA/Stable	Affirmed
Louisville Pkg Auth of River City (Louisville & Jefferson Cnty Metro Govt)		
1st mtg rev bnds ser 2010A-B		
Long Term Rating	AA/Stable	Affirmed
Louisville Pkg Auth of River City (Louisville & Jefferson Cnty Metro Govt)		
1st mtg rev bnds (louisville & Jefferson Cnty Metro Govt) ser 2013A due 06/		
Long Term Rating	AA/Stable	Affirmed
Louisville Pkg Auth of River City (Louisville & Jefferson Cnty Metro Govt)		
1st mtg rfdg rev bnds (louisville & Jefferson Cnty Metro Govt) ser 2013B du		
Long Term Rating	AA/Stable	Affirmed

Louisville Pkg Auth of River City (Louisville) 1st mtg rev bnds ser 2002 dtd 12/01/2002 due 06/01/2003-2018 2020 2022 2026 2029 2032

In a very broad sense there are two types of essential service municipal bonds. General obligation bonds, commonly referred to as G.O. bonds, are typically issued to finance the projects a municipality may provide to its residents. This category includes streets, schools, basic infrastructure, police and fire protection. The other broad category is the revenue bond sector and would typically include water and sewer services, electric power, and many other specific city functions that are financed by a specific revenue stream. The bond issue is classified by where the ultimate source of repayment will come from. For instance, a city may collect a sales tax on retail purchases. This sales tax may go to pay for a school or road construction but it is considered a sales tax revenue bond. The sales taxes are pledged to the bondholders and therefore this bond is in the revenue bond sector, even though the tax collections are spent for the overall benefit of the citizens. There are positives and negatives to each sector. General obligation bonds are backed by the full faith and credit of the municipality. This financial support will consist of many different types of revenues and expenses. Predominately, the largest support will be derived by property taxes levied on residential and commercial property. This tax bill is what you pay either through your mortgage payments or directly to the municipality where the property resides. A municipality may have many different line items of income and expenses. A general obligation bond is where you will typically see the pension obligations reside, a hot topic of late. In the revenue bond sector, the number of line items is usually much smaller. There is typically one specific revenue source pledged for the repayment of the bonds issued to finance the project. One example is a water authority for a specific municipality. On a monthly basis you may receive a water bill based on your usage. This bill would include flushing the toilets and watering the lawn. It may also include the cost of how much waste water you produce by flushing those same toilets. The monthly bill you and your fellow residents pay is probably the only revenue source for this type of financing.

As mentioned earlier, a general obligation or revenue bond both have positives and negatives. A general obligation bond is backed by a wide variety of revenue sources but is also more difficult to analyze for this exact same reason. A revenue bond may be easier to analyze but the bondholder is relying on a narrower source of income to repay the debt. Each of the sectors posses many nuances, but ultimately you are attempting to gauge the potential for the municipality to repay its debt. The overall economic climate may also affect the decision making process when evaluating the two sectors. If property values are declining quickly as in 2008 and 2009, avoiding the general obligation debt of an effected municipality may be prudent. As property values decline, so will the property tax revenues associated with the municipality. Prior to the financial crisis of 2008 a portfolio manager may have had a sector distribution of 65% G.O., 35% revenue bonds as a target allocation. Post crisis it may have been prudent to reallocate to 35% G.O., 65% revenue over a period of a couple of years. With the extreme drop in home prices over this period in certain areas of the country, it was extremely important to recognize the potential risk, and take action prior to the actual drop in revenues. Generally, this drop in property tax revenues happens over time due to the way a municipality collects the tax revenue. Homes are not reappraised every year in most cases. Therefore, the drop in revenue happens gradually. This usually gives the bondholder a sufficient amount of time to exit the position. Since the ratings agencies are typically slow to react with a downgrade, the potential exists to obtain a reasonable price on the sale.

The beauty of municipal finance is that many sources of revenue coming into a municipality do not rise or fall overnight. In fact, most of the revenues and expenses tend to move quite slowly and evolve over time. There will usually be plenty of red flags prior to a downgrade in ratings or quality. Using a little common sense can go a long way towards keeping the credit quality intact. After the events in 2008, just looking at your holdings could reveal a great deal about credit. If I owned a general obligation bond in Miami or Las Vegas perhaps I should see a potential red flag. Home prices were falling more than the market and foreclosures were higher than other parts of the country. Predicting a drop in tax revenues would not be particularly difficult even for an inexperienced investor. Depending on the maturity of the holding perhaps moving out of harm's way is a corrective strategy to be employed. Thinking at a macro level can help you foresee many future risks. Just try to connect the dots using your own knowledge of very basic economic principles. In an economic downturn what types of revenue sources might drop faster than others? As the economy begins to weaken, one of the first areas affected is the consumer. In order to protect his or her household finances, the consumer will begin to cut back on discretionary spending. The type of bond this would affect quite quickly is a sales tax revenue bond. In fact, this revenue stream can be more volatile than most municipal income sources. The ratings agencies realize this and factor the volatility into the ratings model. Just like the property tax example above, if the economy takes a sharp turn south as in 2008, an analysis of your sales tax revenue bonds may be prudent. Weed out the lower rated credits that may be susceptible to a drop in revenues.

Practically speaking, we would suggest that most investors need a game plan to attempt to gauge municipal credit quality within their portfolios, particularly portfolio holdings of individual bonds. At the time of purchase request a copy of the ratings report. Make a note of the way the debt is going to be serviced over time. Is it through the collection of a sales tax, property tax, water bill, or other revenue source? Make note of the current rating, and as time passes, try to focus on macro economic trends and relate it back to the portfolio holdings. Take some time at least annually and simply do a internet search for each municipality. Look for news you think could negatively affect the municipality. If possible access the financial statement and see if they operate on a balanced budget. There is a great deal of information in the Management Discussion and Analysis section of the financial statement. It is typically not difficult to read and will give you an idea of how the entity has done financially over the past year or years. It may even give you a glimpse into the future. Treat your bond holdings as you do an equity position. If you own General Motors stock and news breaks of a large vehicle recall, most investors will realize there are potential ramifications to the holding. Try to apply the same fundamental analysis to your bond holdings, and I am confident you will quickly build a much more thorough understanding of what you own and how it may be affected. The key is to simply get your mindset to a point of questioning the logic or thesis for owning the position in the first place.

CHAPTER 3

Maturity Selection

Maturity selection is a critical part of the portfolio construction process. In a high quality fixed income portfolio, it will be a significant factor in the overall yield the portfolio will be able to attain. It will also be the single largest factor in the overall price volatility of the portfolio. In simple terms, the longer the maturity selected, the larger the amount of expected price movement or volatility given a change in the overall level of interest rates. If interest rates increase the same amount for a 5 year bond and a 30 year bond, the price and associated value will fall more for the 30 year bond. How much more depends on a number of factors, but for illustration purposes, we will use the concept of duration. The measure of duration will help us attempt to predict what effect a change in interest rates will have on a specific bond. If I own a 30 year maturity bond and interest rates increase a full percentage point, we can expect the value of the bond to drop approximately 17%. For a 10 year bond, the drop in value would equate to approximately 8.5%. For a 5 year bond, the drop in value would equate to approximately 4.5%. In other words, if interest rates were to rise one full percentage point the value of the 30 year bond would drop 3 times as much as a 5 year bond, and roughly 2 times more than the 10 year bond. The illustration points out that a longer term bond has more risk than a shorter term bond. This is commonly referred to as interest rate risk. It is a different type of risk than credit quality risk when you are gauging the overall risk associated with default. Overall maturity length does have a role in the measurement of credit quality risk as it is easier to judge the quality of a bond over a short term time horizon. I can predict with greater certainty what a municipal credit will look like for the next year versus the next 30 years. So where does this leave us as we attempt to balance risk and reward?

In the municipal bond market, the yield curve is nearly always upward sloping. This simply means that the longer I go out in maturity, the higher the yield I may be able to attain at purchase. There is incentive in the form of higher yield levels to extend my maturity date. If I extend, I receive a higher yield, but accept a higher degree of price volatility as well. This is the risk reward balance we are referring to in the previous paragraph. Unfortunately, this risk reward balance is always in flux. For instance, in the current market if I purchase a 5 year bond I may receive a yield of 1.25%. The yield for a 10 year bond is 2.25% or a full percentage point (1.00%) more. In another market environment it may only be a pickup of a half percent (0.50%). Is the maturity extension worth it, and for which environment? The decision has to be made in the context of the individual's risk appetite and the prospect for higher or lower interest rates in the future. The absolute level of interest rates may also be a factor in your decision. In order to narrow the prospective maturity possibilities, we can consider a couple of relevant issues that pertain to municipal bonds. First, nearly all municipal bonds with a final maturity date of greater than 10 years will have an imbedded call feature. A call feature gives the municipality the right to redeem the bond early. For instance, when a bond is issued with a maturity date of 30 years, it will typically have a 10 year call date. Who does this favor? In the municipal market the issuer has all the advantage when it comes to long term bonds. Let's assume a bond is issued with a 30 year maturity and a 10 year call feature at a yield of 4.00%. The bond is issued at face value or par. Let's now assume interest rates increase over the first 10 years of the life of the bond and the call date is now upon us. The issuer will certainly not call the bond since they would have to refinance the debt at a higher rate. Conversely, if interest rates fall they will redeem the bond early and you will be forced to replace the bond at a lower yield than your initial purchase at 4.00%. The deck is stacked in the issuers favor. Another analogy is when you take out a mortgage to purchase a home. If interest rates go up you hold on to the mortgage since it is at an attractive rate. If interest rates fall you simply refinance and get the lower rate. In essence, the municipality has the same degree of control, but the prepayment window is more narrowly defined by the call date. Another factor to consider as we try to narrow our maturity selection horizon is once again the slope of the yield curve. Historically, the yield pickup is very limited once you get past 20 years in maturity length. In our earlier example, we were considering going from a 5 year maturity at a yield of 1.25% to a 10 year maturity at 2.25%, a clear pick up in yield of one full percentage point (1.00%). Let's now consider the maturity extension from 20 to 25 years. In today's market that pickup is less than 0.2%. In other words, if I buy a high quality 20 year maturity bond today the yield is approximately 2.80%. If I extend the maturity to 25 years the yield rises to 3.00%. If I continue to extend to 30 years in maturity the yield is only 3.07%. The yield curve is much flatter in the longer years than in the earlier years and this has been relatively consistent over recent history (30 years). So why don't we use some more of that common sense and choose a maturity range that may be a reasonable balance of risk and reward. If I narrow my choices to eliminate the long maturity bonds due to the call features and minimal yield gain, I am left with what can be characterized as the intermediate maturity range. This is not a clearly defined maturity range, but generally speaking, it is considered to be between 5 and 15 years. In my opinion, the investor seeking a balance of yield and price stability is best suited with an intermediate length portfolio. To further mitigate the risk to the portfolio from rising interest rates, a laddered maturity schedule can be constructed. This bond ladder assigns an amount to be invested in each year or range of years to provide maturing securities on a frequent schedule, thus allowing reinvestment of principal in many interest rate and market environments. It spreads the risk over the expected life of the portfolio. This does not necessarily mean each year is equally weighted out to 15 years. It can be constructed to mirror your interest rate outlook or even plan for an expected portfolio withdrawal down the road.

In all fairness, the shorter intermediate maturity portfolio will typically provide a lower return over time than the longer term portfolio. According to Barclays, the total return for a long term (25 years in maturity) high quality, municipal bond index has annualized at a rate of 5.46% for the most recent decade. Over the same time period, a 10 year municipal index has returned 5.09%. The relatively small drop in total return versus the intermediate portfolio leads us to the following conclusion: The investor seeking income and capital preservation from a fixed income allocation may be best suited with a high quality, intermediate maturity, municipal bond portfolio.

CHAPTER 4

Yield Versus Total Return

Many investors confuse the concepts of Yield versus Total Return within the contexts of municipal bond performance. They are related but entirely different measures of how to judge a bonds value over a given timeframe. The concepts that will be outlined on the following pages will all concentrate more on the yield side of the equation, but in the end it will also have a relationship with the ultimate total return of the portfolio.

When discussing the yield of a bond most investors think of the purchase yield or yield at cost. This is also commonly referred to as the yield to maturity. The yield to maturity of a bond is the yield that a security will return to the investor based on a purchase date, purchase price, coupon rate, and final maturity. This yield will be constant for the life of the bond. If I purchase a bond maturing in 10 years at a yield to maturity of 4.00% and I hold that bond to the maturity date then my yield is 4.00%. The price can go up or down in the meantime, but ultimately I will achieve my yield if held to maturity. This concept is fairly easy to understand for most investors. The problem arises when total return is inserted in to the equation.

The concept of total return is quite different than the concept of yield. The total return of a bond investment is typically for a time period that does not coincide with the purchase date or maturity date. Total return is how most mutual funds illustrate their performance for a certain period. Unlike yield to maturity, total return takes interim price fluctuations in to account when calculating the results. For instance, in the example above we purchased a bond with a yield to maturity of 4.00%. But if we wanted to know the total return of the investment for just one time period, say a year, this will most likely not equate to the yield to maturity. Total return will combine the income produced for that one year period with the beginning and ending price for the same period. It assumes a life for the investment only equal to the time period we are measuring. If I purchase a 4.00% coupon bond at 100 with a final maturity date of 10 years my yield to maturity is 4.00%. If I calculate my total return for the first year of the investment and the price falls over that time period the total return will be a combination of the 4.00% income from the coupon and the loss in value due to the drop in price. The resulting total return for the one year period will be less than 4.00%.

In my opinion, yield is more important than total return for many reasons. Most individual investors buying municipal bonds are looking for income. They do not typically look to the municipal bond portfolio to create total return. They will typically look to the stock market or perhaps a real estate investment to produce a higher return. Municipal bonds are unique in the fixed income markets due to the tax exempt nature of the coupon flows. However, a bond calculation that will measure a change in price does not discriminate between tax exempt or fully taxable bonds. A municipal bond with a 4.00% coupon purchased at 100 maturing in 10 years carries a yield to maturity of 4.00%. A corporate bond with the same characteristics will enjoy exactly the same yield to maturity if purchased at the same price. Why does this matter? If I trade my municipal portfolio in an attempt to deliver more total return, there will be tax consequences versus simply holding the bond to maturity. If I purchase a municipal bond and interest rates fall the price of my bond will most likely go up. As stated earlier the bond calculation does not care if the coupons are tax exempt or not. Therefore, my total return for the time period before tax may be 4.25%, but the after tax calculation will be less due to the capital gain. If I sell at the higher price I have simply converted my future tax exempt coupon payments in to a current taxable gain producing a lower after tax total return. If the portfolio is constantly bled of the higher yielding securities to produce total return, the after tax yield will suffer. This is really only the case for municipal bonds because of the different tax exempt treatment the coupon enjoys. Municipal bonds are almost always purchased in a type of account where the investor is paying taxes. If the investor was not paying taxes, they would probably not have purchased the municipal in the first place. The moral of the story is when evaluating a manager or mutual fund based on published total return performance you need to drill down to determine the after tax total return in order to make a sound judgment. The high turnover manager may produce more headline grabbing total return but the after tax return can be substantially less.

I have always held the belief that concentrating on the yield of a bond will ultimately result in obtaining a higher total return. If I constantly purchase bonds that yield more than the market and hold those bonds to maturity I should outperform from a total return perspective over time. We know this from examining total return calculations historically. Over longer time periods, the total return of a municipal bond investment is mainly derived from the coupon payments received, not the price appreciation or depreciation. Therefore it makes intuitive sense to attempt to maximize the coupons or yield of the portfolio in order to produce a higher total return over longer time periods. These returns will be highly tax efficient as well and not be denigrated on an after tax basis.

In the pages that follow we will investigate many different types of municipal bonds. The common thread between them all is the higher yields they will typically carry versus the market in general. Once again, these higher yields should produce higher total returns over longer time horizons.

CHAPTER 5

The AAA Scale

I n order to further understand the concept of yield in relation to various market climates we can use the concept of the AAA scale. Every day, there are a number of private firms that provide a representative scale of where a high quality AAA rated municipal bond would come to market for a certain maturity. For instance, the scale may indicate that on today's date a AAA rated bond maturing in 15 years would come to market at a yield of 2.75%. This is a hypothetical yield that is not directly tied to a single bond transaction but is a compilation of large institutional trades that have occurred in AAA rated bonds with a maturity of 15 years. This data is aggregated in a maturity order scale from 1 to 30 years in length. At each maturity date on the scale there is a representative yield level that corresponds to that date. Therefore an investor could get a reasonable approximation of where a AAA rated bond would expect to trade from a yield perspective for virtually any maturity on any day. Historical databases exist with this information going back many years. If I was curious where 15 year maturity AAA rated bonds traded from a yield perspective 10 years ago, I can quickly research this information. It is relevant because it gives the average investor access to what an independent firm believes a high quality bond may be worth on a given day. Typically, the different market providers are reasonably close to one another in the approximations.

This data can be useful on many levels. If an investor would like to know what yield levels may be available in the market on a generic basis, the AAA scale can be a great starting point. It can also be a useful guide for an individual investor to ascertain if he or she is receiving relative value on a bond purchase. If an investor is contemplating purchasing a AA rated bond at a yield of 2.00% and the AAA scale for that maturity is 2.10%, then an assumption could be made that the potential purchase is too expensive. You would expect to receive a higher yield for a lower rated bond. Professional investors use the scale to trade the market from a spread perspective. If I purchased Memphis, Tennessee General Obligation bonds at a yield of 25 basis points (0.25%) above the AAA scale for a 10 year maturity, I may assume I can purchase a 12 year bond of the same name at the same spread relationship. It gives you a point of reference in which to extrapolate value for all the various municipal bonds that may be available for purchase on any given day. The municipal market is extremely diverse in the names that trade on a daily basis. The AAA scale can be a very useful guide to level the playing field over time. Let's imagine that on a Monday of a given week, I purchase a AA rated, general obligation Kansas bond maturing in 10 years at a yield of 2.00%. The AAA scale on this day for a 10 year bond was 1.75%, so I received a yield of 0.25% or 25 basis points in excess of the AAA scale. Fast forward to Wednesday of the same week, and I am contemplating the purchase of another AA rated general obligation bond, this one from Ohio. I now have a point of reference to fall back on as I know what spread to the AAA scale I attained on the previous purchase. I can adjust for the nuances in the two bonds, but at least I have a frame of reference from which to make a reasonable valuation decision. In essence, this is how the municipal market works. Every trade is relevant in some way to another trade. Since the same bond does not trade every day, we have to continually extrapolate the relationship from one bond to another. As a municipal professional, the relationship between bonds is the very basis in which you make trading decisions.

From a portfolio management perspective, we use the AAA scale as a way to monetize the value added from our purchases. An individual investor can do the same thing as they analyze new purchase opportunities. We have analyzed hundreds of portfolios at Crawford over the years, and one of the analysis we perform is to calculate what yield an investor attained in the market on an individual bond purchase. We compare the purchase yield to the AAA scale on the day of the transaction. We have found that most individual investors purchasing municipal bonds achieve the yield depicted by the AAA scale, yet rarely are they purchasing AAA rated bonds.

CHAPTER 6

The Effect of De Minimis: Preference for Premiums

This may not sound intuitive, but we are a big proponent of purchasing premium bonds or bonds trading at a price above face value or par. Most of the preferred structures mentioned in this text will trade at a premium to face value, or above par, so I felt I should attempt to illustrate in more general terms why premium bonds are preferable to discount or par bonds. De minimis or market discount is an IRS regulation that affects all municipal bonds and has had far reaching implications for our market, though it is rarely discussed, and many investors have never even heard of it. However, if you point out to most investors that the majority of new issues in the municipal market now come at a premium to face value or are issued at a price above par, they will be aware of this fact. De minimis is the biggest reason why most municipals are issued at a price above

100 or par. Since so many of the preferred structures we discuss are premium bonds, allow me to elaborate on the regulation. The de minimis rule was introduced in the mid 1980s as a way to capture additional tax revenue for the IRS. The rule works like this: every municipal bond is assigned a de minimis threshold price. This price is based on several factors, including the original issue price of the bond and the final maturity of the bond itself. For example let us assume a bond came to market as a new issue at face value or a price of 100 and has the following details:

Today's Date	Description	Coupon	Maturity	Price	Yield
1/1/2014	Muniville (Par or Face Value)	4.00%	1/1/2022	100.00	4.00%

As you can see, the bond has a final maturity date in the year 2022, and matures eight years from today's date. The de minimis threshold price for this bond as of today's date is 98.00. The price is derived by allocating one point in price for every four years of maturity. Thus the threshold price is equal to 100.00 minus 2, or 98.00. Only the IRS could come up with something as genius as this. The threshold price has nothing to do with the quality or market price of the bond, only the final maturity and how many years are remaining to maturity from the current date. So a twelve year final maturity would have a threshold price of 97 and a two year maturity would have a threshold price of 99.50. Now that we have determined how to calculate the de minimis price, we will examine why it matters. Let's assume in our example above that in the current market the bond is worth a yield of 4.00%, which translates to a market price of 100.00.

Let us further assume that interest rates are heading higher and in response, our bond begins to drift down in price. Interest rates increase to 4.30% for our bond and the price drops to 98.01. Remember, our de minimis threshold price is 98.00. The inflection point where the market price and the de minimis price meet is critical. As our market price approaches the de minimis price of 98.00, we need to pay a great deal of attention to the price we are willing to pay for the security in question. Here is why: if you purchase the bond at a price above the de minimis price, say 98.01 and hold the bond to maturity, you will pay a capital gain on the difference between the value at maturity or 100.00 and your purchase price of 98.01. The tax rate will be based on the long term capital gains rate, currently at 23.80%. However, if you purchase the bond at 97.99, or just below the de minimis threshold price of 98.00, the capital gain will be taxed at a rate equivalent to your ordinary marginal tax rate or as high as 43.40%! The purchase price is only pennies different, but the difference in the capital gains rate applied to the discount causes a discrepancy in the actual yield you will earn over the life of the bond. If you pay 98.01, the yield at purchase is 4.30%, and after you pay the capital gains at maturity at a rate of 23.80%, the yield drops to 4.25%. If you purchase the bond at 97.99, your yield is also 4.30%, but the yield after you pay the capital gains at maturity at a rate of 43.40% drops to 4.20%. The market penalizes the bond purchased below the threshold price to equalize the after tax yield. In the case of this example, the bond would have to be purchased at a price of 97.52 in order to earn the same after tax return as the bond purchased at 98.01. In other words, in order to receive the same after tax return, you would need to purchase the bond at a gross yield of 4.37% versus 4.30% to achieve an after tax yield of 4.25%. If interest rates continue to rise and prices fall further the condition worsens because this relationship is exponential.

So how do we avoid this pitfall? We simply purchase premium bonds so we have a larger cushion from a rise in interest rates before we approach the de minimis threshold price. Look at the following example:

Today's Date	Description	Coupon	Maturity	Price	Yield
1/1/2014	Muniville (Premium)	5.00%	1/1/2022	106.79	4.00%

Notice our purchase price is much higher, but our yield is still 4.00%. This is the same yield as our original purchase in the previous example. The de minimis threshold price is the same as in the previous example, or 98.00, because the maturity date is the same. The difference in the two bonds materializes if interest rates rise and the price of the bond begins to fall. In the second example with a premium bond, the price will have to fall much further before the threshold price comes into play. In fact, the bond would have to fall in price 8.79 points in order to reach the de minimis threshold price. In our first example the price had to fall only 2.00 points before the threshold price was reached. The premium bond offers a built in security feature and is why most new issue municipal bonds originate at a premium to face value, because investors demand the structure in order to protect the value of their investment.

In summary, we never want to purchase a security that will drop in price more than the market in general just based on an IRS regulation, especially since we can easily avoid the scenario by purchasing a premium bond.

CHAPTER 7

The State Single Family Mortgage Sector, or "Housing Bond"

T he State Single Family Mortgage bond sector is one of our favorites. The combination of safety of principal, above market yields, low volatility, and inefficient trading make this sector ripe for a municipal bond program. We would like to illustrate in more detail what it is about this sector that attracts us and keeps us coming back for more year after year.

Most states issue municipal debt for state run agencies responsible for lending money to first time homebuyers. The ability for these agencies to issue bonds at a tax free interest rate creates a pool of funds available to first time homebuyers at rates below existing traditional mortgages. The states allocate funds through traditional lenders. The resulting mortgages created are typically 30 year fixed rate structures. Mortgages are only granted to first time homebuyers with a maximum home price equivalent to the median home price for the specific state. The issuers lend money at a positive spread to cover administrative expenses. Loans are serviced by traditional mortgage servicing companies.

The state single family mortgage-backed sector is one of the few sectors in the municipal market that has not experienced a default at the issuer level. The vast majority of issuers are rated AA or AAA on their own merits. The sector has a long history of low default rates on the underlying mortgages due in part to rigid lending standards and potential backing from various forms of government support such as FHA, VA, GNMA, FNMA, and FHLMC. Private mortgage insurance is also utilized in the absence of government support. The underlying assets of the authority are available to make principal and interest payments if needed. Each individual bond series will usually create a debt service reserve at issuance as well. Throughout the housing debacle during and after the great recession, the sector maintained its overall high quality bias. Downgrades have been scarce, and the few that have occurred have been minor. We expect the credit quality to continue to improve as the housing market recovers.

There are several factors that influence the overall yield levels available in this sector. The structure of the securities in this sector is reasonably complex. This is not the typical "plain vanilla" municipal bond with which many market participants are familiar. The municipal market is dominated by retail investors with limited knowledge of more complex municipal structures and additional yield is needed to attract sufficient investors to place the debt. Many mortgage backed municipal issues are also subject to the Alternative Minimum Tax, further confusing the individual investor. We will discuss the Alternative Minimum Tax in more detail in Chapter 17. The typical issue comes to market with a deal size of approximately $50 million. Each issue can be comprised of serial bonds, term bonds, super sinkers, PAC bonds (Planned Amortization Class) or more than likely a combination of all. Confused yet? What do you think happens in the secondary market three years after the original issuance? The reality is no one remembers how the deal was structured and this lack of knowledge can lead to an inefficiently traded security.

There is also a general market perception that all mortgage backed municipal bonds are callable at face value at any time. Many investors ignore the sector based on this perception alone. It is true that as the underlying mortgages prepay, funds will return to the authority and can be used to redeem debt, or in certain instances, the funds can be recycled as new loans to other first time homebuyers. If funds are utilized to redeem debt, any number of scenarios can be present for the allocation of the proceeds in the form of a bond call or redemption. The bond indenture spells out the sequence of the calls. This sequence varies from issuer to issuer, and no two are alike. Some issuers call bonds only from within an individual series while others "cross call" from all outstanding series. The possibility of any one maturity being called is dependent on many different factors. The structure of the original deal (super sinkers, PAC bonds, etc.) is a determining factor as well. A market perception that a maturity can be called at whim by the issuer may be very far from reality. It requires a great deal of research to identify the call risk with each particular issue. This information can be gathered by reading the indenture, utilizing issuer websites, and actually calling the issuers. There is no central repository to locate this information, which frustrates potential purchasers. Most market participants will not go to this length to uncover the information. Therefore, most investors will not pay a premium to face value in order to protect themselves from an unanticipated call at face value, no matter how high the coupon on the security in question. For instance a 5.00% coupon bond with a 10 year maturity may be intrinsically worth a price of $112.00 and a yield of 3.50%, but because of the unknown redemption status the actual market price paid is $104.00, producing a yield of 4.50%. This of course leads to the possibility of acquiring an extremely cheap (high yielding) high quality fixed income asset. It also leads to an asset that exhibits very low price volatility as compared to the general market.

Low volatility also plays a part in the defensive characteristics of single family housing bonds. From an historical perspective, the total return on housing bonds will typically outperform versus other high grade sectors of the municipal market during periods where interest rates are rising. There is a distinct difference in the ability of this sector to produce downside protection in periods of rising interest rates.

Case Study on Housing Bonds
Transaction Date: August 24, 2010

On August 24, 2010, Municipal Securities Rulesmaking Board trade data reveals a trade occurred for the issuer Alaska

State Housing Finance Authority. This issuer raises funds through the issuance of municipal bonds and then extends mortgage money to veterans for the purchase of single family residences within the state of Alaska. The mortgages are guaranteed by GNMA, FNMA, or FHLMC. Based on these ultimate guarantees, the ratings agencies award the bonds a rating of AAA. In addition, the state of Alaska fully guarantees the veterans program securities and the state carries a rating of AA. The combination of guarantees provides a very high issuer credit quality threshold and is well suited for an investment program targeted to high quality. This sector of the municipal marketplace typically displays a great deal of trading inefficiency due to the structural characteristics of the underlying security. There is a perceived risk of early redemption or call with nearly all housing bonds, including this one. Generally speaking, investors are unwilling to pay a premium to face value for fear of having bonds redeemed at 100% of face value, virtually at any time. Therefore, even above market coupon bonds will trade at only a slight premium to face value due to the overriding prospect of an early call. In reality, the call or redemption risk can typically be identified through extensive research, and the risk can then be quantified.

Based on data available from the Alaska agency's own website, many of the underlying mortgages that were originated from proceeds of the bond issue had already prepaid. This would usually lead to a redemption in the bond issue in order to maintain parity between program assets (mortgages) and liabilities (bonds). However, the website data indicates little if any of the bonds were being called from this particular bond issue. In this case the agency decided to re-lend the proceeds of the existing mortgages that were being paid off instead of retiring existing bonds. The program was experiencing substantial loan demand and the agency does not have the ability to issue new debt to meet the demand. Therefore, as current homeowners paid off the existing mortgages and the agency received cash, they decided to re-lend the funds to new borrowers instead of retiring the outstanding bonds. This is allowed under the indenture and is called recycling. This is extremely important as we now have a security that the market perceives is at risk for early redemption, but in reality there is minimal risk from early redemption for the foreseeable future. This dislocation between perception and reality can create tremendous value for the bondholder.

Description	Coupon	Maturity	Price	Yield
Alaska State Housing Finance Authority	4.90%	6/1/2022	103.50	4.55%

At the time of purchase 10 year U.S. Treasury securities were yielding 2.55%. The Alaska yield at purchase equates to a taxable equivalent yield of close to 7.00% for an investor in the maximum federal income tax bracket, nearly tripling the yield available on the Treasury security. A more "plain vanilla" structure of municipal bonds with the same coupon and maturity date would trade at a yield of 2.00%. Thus, the Alaska bond yield at purchase is 255 basis points higher than the yield available for simplistic structures of high quality bonds of the same maturity. Obviously, the Alaska bond has a much higher earnings potential over the life of the bond. However, if the agency decides to change the current policy regarding recycling the bond issue could be redeemed prior to maturity at face value. This could result in a yield that is far less than the yield if held to the maturity date.

CHAPTER 8

Premium Callable Cushion Bonds

One of the most overlooked sectors in the municipal bond market is the premium callable or cushion bond structure. Many market participants, including portfolio managers, will not employ the resources necessary to fully understand the nuances of this sector. This type of bond structure essentially has two or more potential maturity dates: the call dates and the final maturity date. A portfolio manager attempting to mirror a particular index will avoid this structure due to the uncertainty of the final maturity. This of course leads to a type of bond that is less efficiently traded in the marketplace, and less efficiency typically leads to higher yielding securities. I feel it is well worth the effort of including these structures in a municipal portfolio and believe it is possible to effectively manage the portfolio to all potential maturity dates.

A premium bond is a security that has an above market coupon rate for the ultimate final maturity as compared to other bonds of the same maturity range. Thus, it will trade at a price in the market above face value (premium) due to the higher coupon rate available versus other new issues. If the bond is also callable prior to maturity, it has the potential to be redeemed prior to the ultimate final maturity date. The bond will have multiple potential redemption dates. This is a more complicated bond structure to analyze and attempt to determine a reasonable price to pay. With multiple redemption dates, we need to calculate a yield to the various possible outcomes and compare these yields to other more plain vanilla structures of the same maturity. If a bond has a final maturity of ten years and a call date of five years we will calculate the yield to both of the potential maturity dates. We will then compare those yields to what is available in the market for a five year non-callable bond and a ten year non-callable bond. We will attempt to illustrate this in the chart below.

Purchase Date	Description	Coupon	Maturity	Call Date	Price
7/1/2013	Sample Bond (Premium)	5.00%	7/1/2023	7/1/2018 @ 100	$114.20

Yield to 5 year call date in 2018: **2.00%**
Yield to 10 year maturity in 2023: **3.32%**

These yields compare very favorably to the yield available for a non-callable five and ten year maturity bond of the same quality:

Yield to 5 year non-callable bond: **1.00%**
Yield to 10 year non-callable bond: **2.32%**

In this example, a purchaser would gain a full percentage point in yield no matter what maturity actually comes to pass. However, the buyer would not know which maturity scenario would apply until the call date approaches. The risk then lies in the fact that if interest rates rise, the callable bond will not be called, and the bond will extend to the maturity date of ten years. However, the yield will also increase from 2.00% to 3.32%. Due to the increase in yield from the bond not being called, this type of bond is also called a "cushion bond" because it will cushion the effect of a rise in interest rates.

Another way to look at this transaction is to literally separate the bond in to two pieces. The first piece would be a bond that will mature on the call date in 5 years. The coupon rate is 5.00% and the purchase price is $114.20. For this bond we will earn an annualized return of 2.00% if it is called after 5 years. The purchase price will be amortized to the call date and on that date the cost basis will have been written down to the call price or 100. The second piece of the bond in question exists if the bond is not called. It will have a purchase date of 7/1/18 which is the call date. The maturity date will be 7/1/2023 and our purchase price will be our amortized cost basis or 100. For this security the yield is the coupon rate or 5.00%. In essence, my first bond is a 2.00% bond, and the second is a 5.00% bond. The yield actually "steps up" at the call date if it is not called because I have written down my cost basis to 100 by the call date. The second 5 year bond is extremely attractive unless interest rates have risen substantially by the call date. If I blend the two yields (2.00% and 5.00%) the overall yield to maturity from the original purchase date is the 3.32% mentioned earlier.

The portfolio manager must have the ability to manage the municipal portfolio to multiple call dates and potential maturity dates. This is more complicated than managing to a single absolute maturity date, but as you can see, it can be well worth the extra effort.

Case Study for Premium Callable "Cushion" Bonds
Transaction Date: 12/2/2013

Municipal Securities Rulesmaking Board or MSRB trade data reveal a transaction for the following bond. The issuer is the State of Indiana Finance Authority Highway Revenue bonds. The bond issue is rated Aa1/AA/AA+ by the three major ratings services. This particular issue was first originated in 2007. The issue is from the premium callable sector of the municipal market and has essentially two potential maturity outcomes: the call date and the final maturity date. We have illustrated the details below.

Trade Date	Description	Coupon	Maturity	Call Date	Price
12/2/2013	Indiana Finance Authority	4.50%	12/1/2025	12/1/2016 @ 100	$104.257

The bond issue in question has a final maturity date of 2025 and a potential maturity date of 2016, depending on whether the call feature is exercised by the issuer. In our trade analysis, we compared the yield of both potential outcomes of the Indiana Finance bond to the yields currently available if we were to invest in a more simplistic non-callable structure of bonds with a similar maturity date based on our purchase price. We have illustrated this comparison in the chart below:

	12/1/2016	12/1/2025
Indiana Finance Authority	3.00%	4.05%
AAA rated non-callable bond	0.50%	2.95%
Yield Gain	2.50%	1.10%

The yield gain utilizing the Indiana bond is substantial to either maturity scenario as compared to the industry standard AAA municipal yield. The most likely scenario is the bond will be called and our pick up in yield will approximate 250 basis points, versus a AAA-rated non-callable bond maturing in 2016. If interest rates rise from current levels, the bond may not be called and our yield will then increase to 4.05%. This yield is 110 basis points higher than a AAA-rated non callable bond with a maturity date of 2025. The increase in yield if the bond does not get called will help cushion the buyer from the effects of rising interest rates as the maturity date increases to 2025.

CHAPTER 9

Industrial Development Bonds, or IDBs

T he IDB sector of the municipal market is one in which significant dislocations can occur. Typically, this sector will not possess the overall credit quality we seek, but in some instances, we can find a high quality issuer and exploit the inefficiencies inherent with the sector. In essence, an IDB is a corporate bond in disguise of a municipality. In some cases, a municipality may allow a corporation to issue a municipal bond in order to utilize the tax-exempt nature of the financing. This will typically allow a corporation to issue a bond at a lower interest rate and is packaged as an incentive to build a plant or headquarters in a particular city or county. The issuer is the municipality through a conduit authority, and the guarantor is the corporation. Once again, the key is the ability to utilize tax exempt financing and lower the issuance costs. Examples of this type of security are municipalities in competition for an automobile manufacturing facility offering various incentives and financing arrangements in order to attract the investment. In return the municipality will receive additional monetary benefits in the form of higher employment for its residents and potential increases in the tax base.

Case Study on Industrial Development Bonds
Transaction Date: July 9, 2009

MSRB trade data indicates the following trade occurred for Albany, Georgia.

Description	Coupon	Maturity	Price	Yield
Albany Dougherty County, GA	5.30%	5/15/2026	94.10	5.86%

This bond was originally issued in 1998 with Albany, Georgia as the conduit authority. The bond is backed by the full faith and credit of Proctor and Gamble, and is rated AA by both the major ratings agencies. In the corporate debt markets, comparable maturity bonds issued by Proctor and Gamble are trading at a yield of 5.00% and are fully taxable. We have seen this type of dislocation in the IDB sector in the past where a tax-exempt bond is actually trading at a yield in excess of a fully taxable security issued by the same ultimate guarantor. The purchase yield of 5.86% is a taxable equivalent yield of over 9.00% to an investor in the maximum federal tax bracket. In all fairness, we should point out that this particular bond will not enjoy the level of liquidity of a high quality Procter and Gamble corporate bond. However, the yield comparison is compelling in our opinion.

CHAPTER 10

The Case of the Missing Rating

O ver half of the bonds outstanding in the municipal market carry bond insurance. Prior to the financial crisis, the vast majority of the insurers carried a AAA rating and this rating flowed through to the bond issues they insure. If proof of insurance was given to the ratings agencies, the bond was automatically awarded the AAA rating regardless of the quality of the underlying municipality.

Ratings are assigned to municipal bonds on an individual issue basis. Therefore, a bond issued in 2003 will be assigned a rating based on information given in the ratings application process. The ratings given can be based on bond insurance, the underlying quality of the municipality, or both. Prior to the financial crisis, when the insurance companies were rated AAA, many municipalities would choose to pay for only the insurance ratings, and not pay for the underlying rating especially if it was lower than AAA. The municipality simply figured, "why pay for a AA rating when the insurance will give us a AAA."

Because ratings are typically assigned to individual bonds at issuance, there can be discrepancies in the publication of the underlying ratings. A bond issued in 2003 shows no underlying rating but the identical issuer may come to market with a deal in 2010 and choose to have the underlying rating published. Technically, the rating for the issuer on the 2010 deal is only for that deal, but in reality both issues are the same credit quality. When a potential investor retrieves a database showing all the bond characteristics for both deals, the investor would actually see an underlying rating for the 2010 deal but would not see a rating for the 2003 issue.

This can certainly cause confusion and opportunity. After the financial crisis, most of the bond insurers were downgraded repeatedly and most are now rated substantially below the original AAA ratings they once possessed. Only one major insurer that existed prior to the financial crisis still maintains a AA rating at this time. As far as the others, most investors are highly skeptical at assigning any value to the insurance on the bonds they back. If a bond issued in 2003 carried only a rating based on insurance and no underlying rating, the rating today would still be based on the current insurance rating. Many of these ratings are in the BBB category or lower. Some have lost their ratings all together. Some have actually gone out of business and carry no rating at all. So when an investor retrieves information on an issuer from a database, it may show a rating that is based on the insurer and is BBB. What if that same issuer came to market at a later date and was actually rated AA on its own merits? Only the more recent issue would carry the AA rating, if the issuer or municipality chose to not pay for the underlying rating on the older insured bond issue. Naturally, these bonds will trade in the marketplace quite differently, as one is AA rated and the other shows a rating of BBB. With research, an investor can determine if these two issues are of the same quality, but typically most do not go to the trouble.

Case Study for Missing Ratings
Transaction Date: January 12, 2012

MSRB trade data reveals the following details of this bond transaction.

Description	Coupon	Maturity	Price	Yield
Cobb County, GA Coliseum, Series 1993	5.625%	10/1/2026	112.50	4.46%

This issue was first introduced to the market in 1993 to construct the Cobb Galleria exhibit facility and is backed by the revenues generated from a hotel, motel, and liquor tax created by Cobb County, Ga. In 2010 these taxes generated approximately $14,000,000 in revenues, and they are pledged to the bondholders. This produces debt service coverage of approximately 2.20 times, meaning the annual revenues pledged to bondholders will cover the cost of the annual debt by over a factor of 2. Moreover, this is senior debt.

On close examination of our 1993 issue we noticed it is actually insured by The Municipal Bond Insurance Association

(MBIA), and was once rated AAA by the major ratings agencies. MBIA was a casualty of the credit crisis that began in 2008. Municipal bonds insured by MBIA are rated Baa2/BBB as of January 2012, as is the case with the 1993 issue. Because of the original AAA rating provided by MBIA, the issuer did not apply for a rating based on its own merits, or an "underlying rating", when the bond was issued in 1993. A subsequent issue brought to market in 2005 is junior in priority to the 1993 bond. It was also insured by MBIA, but the 2005 issue applied for and received an underlying rating by Standard and Poor's. Based on the current financials of the authority, the 2005 issue underlying rating was upgraded in 2009 by S&P to A+. Remember, the 1993 issue did not have an underlying rating; however, it is senior to the 2005 issue that does carry the underlying rating of A+.

The disconnect we are trying to illustrate is the fact the 1993 bond issue traded on 1/12/2012 at a price of 112.50 which is a yield of 4.46% to the 14 year maturity. On 1/14/2012, a seller received a bid of over 120.00 for the 2005 issue. This bid reflects a full 8% increase in price for a bond that is junior to the series 1993 bond. The bond structures are nearly identical as to coupon and maturity, with the real only difference being the underlying rating.

This dislocation would potentially allow an investor to capture value both in terms of relative and nominal yield. A yield of 4.46% is a taxable equivalent yield of close to 7% for an investor in the maximum federal tax bracket. It is also approximately 150 basis points higher in yield than comparable maturity A-rated municipals. In the current low interest rate environment, this purchase shows exceptional value in our opinion.

CHAPTER 11

Sinking Fund Issues

T he sinking fund sector is one of the more complicated types of municipal bonds that exist in the municipal market. It is generally a type of bond that is only bought and sold by more sophisticated investors who have the capability to analyze the various aspects inherent to the structure. Due to the more limited scope of investors attempting to acquire this type of bond, it tends to trade relatively cheap to the market in general. The benefits of owning this sector can be substantial from a yield perspective. Once again, quality is not the determinant of the relative attractiveness of the bond; it is determined by the structure of the bond issue.

A sinking fund is a regularly scheduled redemption or call of one particular maturity. Instead of the call retiring the entire bond at one point in time, a sinking fund retires a portion of an existing issue. When a bond is originally issued it may have a sinking fund feature. The original bond issue for a specific maturity may have a face value at maturity of $1 million. It matures ten years from today and through the sinking fund feature, $100,000 of the outstanding issue retires each year until maturity. There will actually be ten different calls of $100,000 each over the life of the bond. In our example, this will create an average maturity of approximately five years. The calls are spelled out clearly in the bond indenture and are known in advance of purchase. The typical investor does not know how to treat the sinking fund average maturity versus a plain vanilla bond structure with a final maturity of five years. The yield gain for a sinking fund average maturity versus an outright five year maturity can approach one full percentage point. In our opinion this represents exceptional value and to the investor willing to exploit this very inefficient trading vehicle. The more sophisticated investor possesses the ability to calculate the average maturity of the sinking fund structure. In essence, an investor can purchase a single bond and actually have a built in maturity ladder retiring bonds every year. This structure has an added benefit as well. Having a bond that retires principal each year will smooth out the return pattern by allowing the investor to reinvest proceeds from the sinking fund calls in a variety of market environments over the life of the bond. By investing maturing principal from the sinking fund redemptions the volatility of the overall portfolio can be reduced with the addition of this particular bond structure.

Case Study for Sinking Fund bonds
Transaction Date: October 16, 2008

MSRB trade data shows a transaction taking place on the

following security. As a backdrop, the market at this time was experiencing significant dislocations due to the ongoing financial crisis. Liquidity at this time in the municipal market was challenging and many sellers entered the market attempting to raise cash.

The bond in question is actually backed by US Treasury securities held in escrow for the benefit of the bondholders. The bond was originally issued by the Triborough Bridge and Tunnel Authority, NY, in 1992. This bond was refinanced in 2002 and the escrow was created for the benefit of the bondholders. Once again, the authority's association is in name only and the Treasury securities held on behalf of the bondholders by the Trustee are the ultimate security. The bond is rated AAA based on the Treasury escrow.

Description	Coupon	Maturity	Price	Yield
Triborough Bridge & Tunnel Authority, Series 1992	5.50%	1/1/2017	103.50	4.83%

The distinguishing feature of this particular bond is the sinking fund feature beginning in 2013. The bond issue will be redeemed in annual installments beginning in 2013 through the final maturity of 2017. Based on the sinking fund calls, the average maturity is 11/18/2014. We have displayed the various call dates along with the corresponding yield levels the investor would earn to those calls. For illustrative purposes, we are also showing the yield available for a AAA-rated bond of the same maturity at the call dates.

Sinking Fund Redemption

Date	Purchase Yield	AAA Rated Bond	Spread Difference
2013	4.57%	3.71%	0.86%
2014	4.73%	3.94%	0.79%
11/18/14 (Avg. Mat)	4.83%	3.94%	0.89%
2015	4.84%	4.18%	0.66%
2016	4.92%	4.43%	0.49%
2017 (Maturity)	4.97%	4.65%	0.32%

The yield to the average maturity of 11/18/2014 is 4.83% or a spread of 89 basis points over comparable rated bonds of the same maturity. In our opinion this represents an exceptional value. The sinking fund installments return the principal over a range of years, creating a built in maturity ladder for the portfolio. The additional income generated versus a more plain vanilla type bond structure is significant with what is in essence a tax exempt U.S. Treasury bond. The more complicated structure has led to an inefficiently traded security with exceptional value in our opinion.

CHAPTER 12

Super Sinkers

N ow that we have mastered the sinking fund sector let's explore a similar structure called a super sinker. When a municipal bond issue is structured it will typically have what are called serial maturities and term bonds. Serial maturities are bonds issued in sequence by the final maturity date. A term bond is a maturity date out of sequence and usually larger in amount or size. For instance a bond issue may have serial bonds maturing annually from 1/1/2014 through 1/1/2025 in the amount of $1,000,000 per maturity and then a term bond due 1/1/2030 for $10,000,000 par value. The total par value for the issue would be $12,000,000 serial bonds plus a term bond of $10,000,000 equaling $22,000,000. Depending on the specific project being financed and the source of funds being used to repay the bond issue (debt service) there may be a type of maturity utilized called a super sinker.

Let's envision a municipality that wants to build a bridge. The municipality agrees to levy a toll in order for automobiles to use the bridge, and the toll revenues will in turn be used to service the debt and pay back the bondholders. The municipality issues the bond, builds the bridge, and drivers begin to use the crossing and pay a toll to do so. The bond documents state that any excess toll revenue above and beyond what is required to service the debt will be used to retire or reduce principal on the outstanding bond issue. In essence the excess revenue would be used to pay back the loan early, similar to a home-owner adding additional funds to a mortgage payment in order to pay off the loan earlier than originally scheduled. In order to reduce confusion to the bondholders and even to garner a more favorable interest rate at issuance, the bond issue may be structured with a targeted super sinker maturity. This specified maturity will receive all the excess toll revenues in the form of additional principal payments or redemptions. In our bond structure above the targeted maturity date will be the term bond in 2030. The excess revenues can be forecasted and we can determine the potential for these excess payments to shorten the final maturity date of the bond. If our analysis suspects we will receive an additional $500,000 in revenues per year and these funds are targeted to our super sinker maturity in 2030 the actual maturity schedule would be as follows:

Year	Quantity
2014	$500,000
2015	$500,000
2016	$500,000

2017	$500,000
2018	$500,000
2019	$500,000
2020	$500,000
2021	$500,000
2022	$500,000
2023	$500,000
2024	$500,000
2025	$500,000
2026	$500,000
2027	$500,000
2028	$500,000
2029	$500,000
2030	$2,000,000

Instead of receiving only our interest payments and a single final maturity payment in 2030, we will receive annual principal pay downs and then a final payment of $2,000,000 in 2030. The average maturity date will actually be approximately 2023 when all the early maturity redemptions are considered. In actuality, we will develop a range of possible excess principal payments and then apply the results to a range of potential maturity outcomes. Unlike the sinking fund bond in the previous chapter, the super sinker will have a variable outcome and is not set in stone. If fewer people use the toll bridge, our redemptions will be less. Conversely, if more people use the bridge than forecast, the redemptions will be greater. The key is all the excess revenues are targeted to the single maturity date.

Case Study for Super Sinkers
Transaction Date: 6/20/2013

MSRB trade data indicates the following transaction has taken place. The issue in question is from the super sinker sector of the municipal market. The issuer is Little Rock, Arkansas and at the time of issuance the bond is rated Aa2/AA by the major ratings agencies. The bond is backed by sales tax revenues collected within the city. The details of the specific transaction are as follows:

Description	Quantity	Coupon	Maturity	Price
Little Rock, Arkansas Sales Tax Rev. Series 2013	$2,975,000	2.375%	4/1/2028	97.266

The unique feature of this issue is the super sinker structure that will be utilized to retire the bond issue. The bond issue in question will be repaid by the sales tax revenue collected by the city of Little Rock. Based on historical sales tax collections the anticipated debt service coverage will be 1.45 times. The minimum amount of revenues needed to service the debt is obviously 1.0 times; therefore there is a cushion available to the bondholders. The city has pledged to use any excess revenues to retire existing debt early. Based on the projections we can anticipate the 2028 super sinker maturity to begin paying principal in 2017 on the following schedule:

Year	Quantity
2017	$495,000
2018	$2,025,000
2019	$455,000

The average maturity based on this schedule will be 1/25/2018 and the yield to this date is 3.70%. If an investor were to purchase a AAA-rated, non-callable bond in 2018 the yield in today's market would be 1.38%. The gain in yield is in excess of 230 basis points! Due to the long history of sales `tax collections there is an excellent likelihood there will be excess revenues available to meet the redemption schedule above. It would be prudent for an investor to monitor the sales tax flows as new collection data is available via disclosure statements made by Little Rock. This will allow the investor to make alterations to the anticipated maturity schedule as necessary.

CHAPTER 13

Put Bonds

T he put bond sector of the municipal market has evolved into one that can take several shapes and forms. Originally, a put bond was a bond structure where the bond holder controlled the maturity date to a degree by having the ability to "put" the bond back to the issuer on specific dates and prices. It is, in a sense, the opposite of a call feature that can be used by an issuer to redeem a bond earlier than the final maturity.

Over the past 20 years the vast majority of municipal bonds issued with a put feature are now mandatory in nature. The customer or holder of the bond no longer has the option of redeeming the bond as the redemption is mandatory. Thus, a bond may hold a final maturity of 20 years, but is subject to a mandatory put (redemption) in five years. The holder simply has his bonds redeemed in five years and no longer has an option to hold the security past the mandatory redemption or put date. This type of structure can cause a degree of confusion in the market and this leads to a more inefficiently traded security. As we stated prior, this tends to lead to a higher yielding security for the investor who is inclined to do the extra amount of research on the put feature language within the bond indenture.

Why would an issuer want to bring a bond to market with this feature versus a more plain vanilla structure? In the example above, why not just have a bond that matures in five years? Many issuers may desire to structure a bond with a 20 year or longer amortization or payout structure but would also like to take advantage of the slope of the municipal market yield curve. Typically, a longer maturity bond will yield more than a shorter maturity bond. This is the often mentioned yield curve for municipal bonds. An issuer may choose to offer a 20 year bond but the mandatory put feature enables them to take advantage of an interest rate more akin to a five year bond and lower the interest rate they have to pay. At the end of the first five year period, the issuer determines whether to reissue or remarket the bonds as another five year bond or even a different maturity depending on their outlook for interest rates and the overall level of rates at the time of the remarketing. The issuer is able to streamline the issuance process at the put date and the costs are relatively small compared to a complete new issuance of the debt. The bondholder will enjoy a higher yield as compared to a plain vanilla five year bond. It is important for the bondholder to understand the nuances of the put feature language in the indenture, as they vary from issuer to issuer.

Case Study on Put Bonds
Transaction Date: 4/25/2011

MSRB trade data reveals the following transaction. The issue is from the put bond sector of the municipal market. The issuer in question is the Private College and University Authority of Georgia. The financing is for the Agnes Scott College in Decatur, GA. The issue is rated AA by Standard and Poor's and Fitch ratings services. The security for the bond issue is the full faith and credit of Agnes Scott, including a significant endowment. The details are as follows:

Description	Coupon	Put Date	Final Maturity	Price	Yield
Private College & University Series 2011	2.55%	6/1/2015	6/1/2028	100	2.55%

The bonds will bear interest at a rate of 2.55% until the mandatory put occurs on 6/1/2015. On this date the bond will be remarketed at a rate and maturity to be determined. For this analysis, the bond will mature on 6/1/2015 at a redemption price of 100. The complexity of this security will lead to higher than market yields as compared to a more generic four year final maturity fixed rate bond. Currently, a four year generic bond of this quality would be available in the market at a yield of approximately 1.45%. The yield pickup is over 100 basis points and in our opinion this is extremely attractive. In all fairness, the liquidity will not be as high as a generic four year bond, but the issue is expected to enjoy a significant following in the secondary market. At the put date in 2015 the bond will effectively mature for the current bondholders. It will then be remarketed to new owners with a new put date sometime in the future.

CHAPTER 14

Pre-refunded Candidates

I n the municipal market nearly all debt issued beyond a maturity of ten years has an imbedded call feature. Typically, this call feature is ten years in length from the date of issue and gives the issuer the ability to pre pay or to redeem the particular bond at the call date and call price. For example, a 20 year final maturity bond issue would typically possess a call or redemption feature in ten years at a price of 100 or face value. We addressed the premium callable sector in Chapter 4. We will now take that sector one step further and attempt to uncover the pre-refunding candidate which is a type of premium callable bond.

A municipality wishing to retire outstanding high coupon debt has several options. The first option is to wait until maturity or until a bond call can be exercised per the indenture and then replace the issue with a new issue with lower cost debt. One additional way to retire high cost debt is through a process called pre-refunding. In a pre-refunding transaction, a new bond issue is brought to market at prevailing interest rates. The proceeds from the transaction are used to purchase U.S. Treasury securities. The Treasury securities are then placed in an irrevocable escrow account, and they are scheduled to mature when the old high coupon bond is available for call. For instance, if a municipality has a bond outstanding with a 5.00% coupon, 20 year maturity date, and five year call date, it may want to retire the debt from its books. A new issue is brought to market with a new coupon of 3.00%, a potential interest rate savings of 2.00% (5.00% minus 3.00%). Proceeds from the new bond issue are used to purchase U.S. Treasury securities which are then placed in an escrow account. The escrow account is structured in order to have sufficient funds to pay interest on the old bond issue along with the full principal value on the call date. In our example the escrow would be structured to pay coupon interest and then to call the bonds in five years. The municipality has deemed to have retired the old bond with the escrow account.

The marketplace for pre-refunded bonds is highly liquid and efficient due to the certainty of maturity and quality of the escrow account. The pre-refunded sector is extremely large and well followed. One strategy is to identify and purchase municipal bonds prior to the pre-refunding process taking place. After the pre-refunding, the bond issue being retired typically trades at a much lower yield resulting in what can be a substantial price gain. This is due to the bond now having a certain maturity date and the quality of a US Treasury bond. There are a number of factors that influence whether a municipality will choose to pre-refund outstanding debt. These include the original cost of the debt (interest rate), the structure of the call date and price, and the current market for U.S. Treasury securities. There are also IRS regulations involving the transactions that affect whether it is a viable cost savings vehicle. The IRS will only allow a municipal issuer to pre-refund a bond issue one time. This is because the pre-refunding transaction is in essence creating additional tax exempt debt due to the new bond issuance and the old bond remaining outstanding until the call date. Therefore it is necessary to identify whether a bond has used its one time opportunity or if the option remains. An eligible bond will typically be described as a "new money" issue because it was brought to market to finance a new project versus retire an old bond issue. A bond that is issued in order to create the pre-refunding bond is called a "refunding" issue.

Case Study on Pre-refunding Candidates
Transaction Date: March 31, 2010

MSRB trade data indicated the following transaction has taken place in March of 2010.

Description	Coupon	Maturity	Price
Sanford, FL Water & Sewer Revenue Bonds, Series 1993	4.50%	10/1/2021	97.10

On March 31, 2010 a trade was executed on the above referenced security. There are several interesting features of this particular bond that cover several topics we have already discussed in previous chapters. The issue was originally insured by AMBAC, which was a victim of the financial crisis due to exposure to structured financial products, mainly subprime loans. Once rated AAA by both ratings agencies, the insurance is now deemed virtually worthless by many investors. The issuer does carry an underlying rating of A+ by Fitch ratings, and had undergone a recent credit review by the agency. The market in general treats many of these issuers with low regard due to a lack of easily obtainable ratings research information. However, research indicates a reasonable level of security in the issuer, as depicted by underlying ratings and financial data for the authority. The issuer had the ability to refinance the debt with a lower interest rate as early as June of 2010. By comparing the interest rates where similar quality and maturity bonds were being issued to the Sanford bond an educated guess could be made concerning whether the issuer would choose to retire the debt early at 100 or the call price. If the bond issue is called a gain from the purchase price would be realized. If the bond is not called the investor would have the opportunity to hold the debt to maturity. The yield to the maturity date is sufficient to warrant the purchase on its own merits. A call at par would simply be icing on the cake at this point.

The factors the investor had to make were numerous for this security. The issue of whether the bond would be called or remain outstanding was one criteria for purchase. The issue of a lack of a published rating was a second criteria that had to be examined. This is an example of a type of bond that actually falls in to several of the categories we are illustrating in this publication.

CHAPTER 15

30 Day
Callable Bonds

I n previous chapters we have addressed several different types of callable bonds. In this chapter we will investigate a type of callable bond that has one distinguishing call characteristic. The 30 day callable bond is literally that: it can be redeemed by the issuer 30 days from the purchase date. When a municipal bond is issued it will typically have many different maturity dates within the one total bond issue. Nearly all bonds with a maturity date of greater than ten years will have an embedded call feature whereas the issuer has the right to redeem the bond at their option on the call date. This call date is usually ten years from the issue date. For instance, a 15 year maturity will have a call date after ten years from issuance. If we fast forward ten years to a point in time when the call date approaches, the bond will have only five years left until it matures. In essence, we have now reached the original call date as spelled out in the bond indenture. From this date until the final maturity, the bond can be redeemed at a specified price, most often at 100 or face value.

So why would this type of bond be attractive? The issuer has the ability to take this bond away after giving us only 30 days' notice. Isn't that a bad thing? Nearly all municipal bond redemptions or calls are funded through the issuance of a new bond. The proceeds of the new bond are used to pay off the existing debt much like we would get a new mortgage on our home to refinance a higher interest rate mortgage. However, municipal bonds are not always efficiently managed by the municipalities that issue the debt. There are many circumstances where even if it makes economic sense to redeem the bonds on the earliest call date, it does not happen. In our example let's assume the bond was issued when interest rates were higher. At the time of issuance, a 15 year bond was marketed with a 5.00% coupon rate. In the current market, new issue bonds will carry only a 3.00% rate, so it would make economic sense to redeem the old high interest rate debt and replace it with the new lower rate debt. The municipality would save 2% per year in interest costs. But what if the issuer involved is a smaller less sophisticated issuer that comes to market very infrequently. There is the possibility they do not call the bond issue on the first available call date or not at all. But once again, why is this attractive to us as a potential bond purchase. On any given day there will be sellers of this structure of bond. The market is well aware of the potential for a call within 30 days so even if the coupon is high or above current market rates, a potential buyer is not going to be willing to pay much above face value or the call price. This will typically lead to a yield to the first 30 day call of around 0%. However, if the bond is not called, after 60 days, the yield for that period jumps considerably and is now closer to 1.00%. If the bond is not called for 90 days, the yield jumps to 2.00%. For 120 days, the yield now approaches 2.50%. The longer the bond stays outstanding, the more the yield continues to increase, with the largest gain in the early stages. Because of the higher than market coupon rate the price continues to hover close to face value or the call price. Depending on the coupon rate, the market price will remain very constant barring a substantial spike in interest rates. The combination of an ever increasing yield and stable market value make this type of bond very attractive especially for an investor attempting to mitigate risk or insulate a portfolio from the effects of rising interest rates.

The process involved to call a bond is well known. Typically an issuer will bring a new bond to market and use the proceeds to effect the call on the old bond. The process to bring a new issue generally takes a minimum of 90 days to complete. There is no such thing as a shelf registration in the municipal market whereas an issuer can quickly bring a new deal to market. The issuer has to apply and receive ratings, hire underwriters and bond attorneys, and then schedule the issue well in advance to bring it to market. This process is very public and research can typically uncover whether the process has begun. This gives us a window from which we can formulate an opinion on the likelihood of an imminent call.

Case Study for 30 Day Call Bonds
Transaction Date: 08/29/2009

MSRB trade date indicates a trade on the following security in August of 2009.

Description	Coupon	Maturity	Rating
Raleigh County, WV Building Auth, Series 1999	5.375%	10/1/2025	AA

This AA-rated bond was originally issued to build a DMV site for the state of West Virginia in Raleigh County. The bond issue is guaranteed by the state through lease rental payments made to the authority sufficient to pay principal and interest on the bonds. The unique feature of this issue is that it is callable at any time given 30 days' notice by the issuer. Due to the current level of interest rates for this quality and maturity of bonds the issuer could potentially issue new bonds at a lower interest rate and use the proceeds to redeem the 1999 issue and save money over the remaining life of the bond issue. Based on the MSRB reported purchase price we have illustrated the potential yield scenarios:

Call Date	Yield
10/01/2009	0.00%
11/01/2009	2.47%
12/01/2009	3.38%
01/01/2010	3.84%
07/01/2010	4.69%

All of these potential yield levels represent a substantial yield gain as compared to a more generic bond of the same maturity. The investor has essentially accepted a market yield of 0% for 30 days in exchange for the possibility of an extremely attractive yield if the bond is not called for some time. Because of the above market coupon rate, there is little downside price risk, barring a substantial spike in interest rates over the next several years. Interest rates would have to increase to over 5.375% (coupon rate on the bond) for a 2025 maturity before the bond would be at risk of trading to a discount to par value, unless of course the issuer defaulted on its obligations.

In our opinion this type of bond is very attractive based on the opportunity to earn well above market yields while enjoying low price volatility. You may ask why there are actually sellers of this structure of municipal bond. In times of market stress the sector holds its price very well and offers a seller a source of liquidity he may not find elsewhere within his portfolio.

CHAPTER 16

Zero Coupon Municipal Bonds

Zero coupon municipal bonds can be attractive under certain circumstances. Overall, the more common structures of zero coupon bonds present challenges for the risk-averse investor. The lack of an income stream makes this type of bond more price volatile than a coupon bearing bond of the same maturity. The price volatility of a zero coupon bond also increases as the maturity date lengthens.

An investor can derive value from this bond structure depending on market conditions at the time of purchase. Several different avenues for value can be pursued. First, the vast majority of zero coupon issuance in the municipal market is for longer dated bonds, typically maturing from ten years and out. At times, an issuer may feel it is advantageous to issue bonds with a shorter maturity profile. If this issuance is concentrated within certain maturities, value can be derived from an oversupply situation. Typically, a zero coupon bond within the intermediate maturity spectrum (one to ten years) will yield approximately 25 to 50 basis points above the yield of a coupon bearing bond of the same quality and maturity. At times, when sufficient supply hits the market at one time, this spread will widen considerably. Purchasing during this type of market environment can lead to the creation of value for the investor holding to maturity or looking for short term appreciation. It has been our experience that this spread can widen to 50-100 basis points at the time of issuance if there is insufficient demand at the time of pricing. We feel this additional spread or yield is sufficient to offset the price volatility associated with the zero coupon sector. Holding the purchase to maturity will negate the volatility issue to some degree as the bond ages naturally. Waiting for the oversupply situation to correct can also provide short term appreciation as the purchase spread reverses and tightens back to more normal levels. For instance, if a zero coupon bond is purchased at a yield premium of 100 basis points and three months later the spread drops back to 50 basis points, the appreciation on a relative basis is 50 basis points. This can be a substantial amount of gain for a short term time period. That gain can be realized or the additional yield can be harvested for the life of the bond.

A second way a zero coupon bond can be exploited is if it contains any of the other structural characteristics discussed in the previous chapters. Zero coupon bonds can be callable, have sinking funds, have missing ratings, or any other structural anomaly we have already investigated. When you add multiple layers of complexity to a municipal bond the result almost always means additional yield can be available. In our case study for zeros we will give an example of several situations where value can be extracted in the form of higher yields.

Case Study #1 for Zero Coupon Bonds
Transaction Date: July 27, 2009

MSRB data indicates a trade of the following security occurred in July of 2009.

Description	Amount	Coupon	Maturity	Rating	Price	Yield
Coppell, Texas	$1,000,000	0.00%	8/15/2016	AA	76.407	3.90%

An investor may choose to purchase zero coupon bonds when they can add value versus a more traditional coupon bearing bond when this sector becomes cheap relative to the market in general. Zero coupon municipals in the five to seven year range will typically trade at a yield concession of 25 to 50 basis points above current coupon bonds of the same maturity. In this case, the spread was 90 basis points as compared to current coupon bonds of the same issue. This situation will typically occur due to an oversupply situation in the sector, as was the case here. In this case the bonds reverted to more normal levels as compared to coupon bearing bonds within 90 days of the transaction date. The investor can choose to harvest this relative out performance by selling the security or simply enjoy the additional yield from the purchase date to the final maturity.

Case Study #2 for Zero Coupon Bonds
Transaction Date: March 25, 2013

MSRB trade data reveals the following transaction occurred on March of 2013.

Description	Coupon	Maturity	Rating	Price	Yield
Lake County, Illinois Series 2000	0.00%	12/1/2017	NR	90.25	2.20%

Prior to the financial crisis, most bond insurers were rated AAA by the rating agencies. Many municipalities did not apply for an underlying rating due to the fact it may have been lower than the AAA insurance rating and also because of the extra costs involved. After the financial crisis, many of the bond insurance companies suffered mightily, and most have seen their ratings downgraded repeatedly. The bond above was issued for Lake County, Illinois in 2000 and was insured by MBIA. At the time of issuance, the rating based on the insurance was AAA, and the issuer chose to not apply for the underlying rating. At the time of the transaction, the parent company of MBIA had recently downgraded to the BB category, or junk status.

We feel it is imperative to purchase municipal bonds based on the underlying credit and not based on bond insurance or other types of credit enhancement. It is important to look to the underlying ability of the issuer to make debt service payments. Underlying ratings can assist us in our investment decision to acquire a bond, but further research in to a municipalities finances is always a good idea. For the bond in question, we refer you back to the chapter titled "The Case of the Missing Ratings". Municipal bonds are somewhat unique in that ratings are assigned to individual issues, not to the issuer in general. Therefore, an issue that came to market in 2000 may not have an underlying rating, but a subsequent issue brought in 2010 may have applied and received an underlying rating. The two issues have the same lien on the revenues from the municipality and are actually parity debt, but one issue is rated and the other is not. The databases in the public domain will show the published ratings for each and in this particular case the 2000 bond issue now shows as nonrated, due to the demise of MBIA and the fact they did not apply for an underlying rating. In actuality, the issuer received a ratings upgrade by Standard and Poor's in February of 2013. The underlying rating was upgraded from AA- to AA. The rating upgrade was due to solid financial performance the past four years, strong cash balances, and high resident income levels. So in reality, the 2000 bond issue is of AA quality. In the inefficient municipal bond market, this security is at a significant discount to what we would call fair value.

In today's low interest rate environment, a four year AA-rated zero coupon municipal bond would yield 1.25%. The transaction purchase yield of 2.20% is nearly a full percentage point above this level. That equates to a taxable equivalent yield of 3.67% for an investor in the 40% tax bracket. Comparable maturity U.S. Treasury notes are currently yielding 0.55%, and in our opinion makes this an exceptional purchase.

Once again, multiple layers of inefficiency are apparent in this transaction. First the zero coupon structure is more complex in nature than a straight coupon bearing instrument. Secondly, the missing rating complicates the issue and makes the quality determination that much more difficult. The yield gain however is in our opinion worth the extra effort.

CHAPTER 17

Alternative Minimum Tax Subject Municipals

S ometimes the structure of a bond comes in a different form than the coupon, call date or maturity date. AMT-subject municipals are not a particular structure of bond but a sector that is taxed differently than a "regular" municipal bond. The interest from an AMT-subject municipal bond is taxed at a rate of 28% if the individual that owns the bonds is subject to the Alternative Minimum Tax.

AMT-subject municipals came into existence in 1986. They are also sometimes referred to as "private activity" bonds. The AMT status is derived from the underlying project that is being financed. For example, if a municipal bond is issued for the purpose of financing an airport or a port improvement, more than likely it will be issued as a private activity bond and interest paid to bondholders will be subject to the AMT tax, if the bondholder is subject to the tax. It is not the source of the bond guarantor that determines the AMT status; it is the underlying project. For example, if the Port of Houston, Texas issues debt for port improvements, it is most likely AMT subject, even though the debt is guaranteed by Harris County, Texas and is AAA rated.

Municipal bonds subject to the Alternative Minimum Tax (AMT) are consistently undervalued and offer considerable value for certain high income investors. Those who are capable of capitalizing on this fixed income investment vehicle have an opportunity to earn substantially higher yields on their municipal bond investments. The simple reason AMT-subject issues are so attractive is because few bond buyers truly understand them. This leads to less demand, which in the bond market typically translates to additional yield. In short, the inefficiency exists because the vast majority of buyers of municipal bonds avoid issuers that are subject to the alternative minimum tax out of fear that they (or their clients) will be subject to a 28% tax rate on what is otherwise a tax-exempt bond. While paying tax on a tax-exempt issue is typically not desirable, in many cases the excess yield offered by AMT-subject municipals leads to a superior after-tax yield, even for those investors who do fall into the AMT bracket. However, the real opportunity is for those higher income earners paying marginal tax rates well above the 28% AMT rate and are not subject to the AMT.

Over the past ten years, we have seen a substantial increase in the relative value of Alternative Minimum Tax-subject municipals. As more American taxpayers become subject to the tax, many avoid AMT-subject bonds, leading to a favorable price and yield differential for those who have an ability to earn

AMT-subject income. This investment is well suited for the individual that has high amounts of ordinary income and is unlikely to be subject to the AMT tax. The incremental yield available for AMT subject municipals can range from an additional 25 basis points to more than 100 basis points of additional yield, depending on market conditions.

One additional advantage is a possibility for future comprehensive tax reform that eliminates the AMT tax altogether. This could lead to an increase in the value of our investment as the AMT stigma is removed. We would expect the bonds to increase in price as the yield drops to the level of non-AMT subject bonds of the same maturity and quality. In all fairness, we should also point out that an AMT- subject bond will not enjoy the same amount of liquidity as a non-AMT bond. However, we find most investors of short-to-intermediate maturity bonds typically hold them to maturity. Thus the minor lack of liquidity is negated as bonds edge closer to maturity each year. We would also caution the unsophisticated investor from employing this strategy without the assistance of a professional bond manager with expertise in the AMT sector due to the trading nuances of this type of municipal bond.

Case Study for AMT Subject Municipals
Transaction Date: October 15, 2013

MSRB trade data reveals the following trade occurred in October of 2013. The issuer is the Port of Houston Texas and the guarantor is Harris County, Texas. These AAA-rated bonds are a general obligation of Harris County and backed by the full faith and credit of the municipality. The unique aspect of this transaction is the bonds are classified as "private activity" bonds by the IRS and are subject to the Alternative Minimum Tax. This means if the purchaser is subject to the AMT, then interest on this bond will also be AMT subject at a tax rate of 28%. Due to the stigma placed on AMT-subject securities, the bonds traded at an extremely attractive yield versus the market in general in our opinion. For the investor that has the ability to utilize AMT-subject municipals the following transactions has yield enhancing benefits. We have listed the details below:

Description	Amount	Coupon	Maturity	Call Date	Rating	Price	Yield
Port of Houston, Texas	$1,200,000	5.00%	10/1 2025	10/1 2006	AAA	107.07	2.50%

The bond has two possible maturity scenarios: the call date in 2016 and the maturity date in 2025. The transaction price produces what we believe to be an attractive yield, no matter which scenario actually happens. The yield to the call date in 2016 is 2.50%. This compares very favorably to other AAA-rated bonds with a 2016 maturity. A non-callable AAA bond with a 2016 maturity would currently be yielding 0.62%. The yield to the final maturity in 2025 is 4.24% versus a 2.95% available for like bonds maturing in 2025. The yield pickup to comparable bonds is 188 basis points to the call date and 129 basis points to the maturity date. A significant amount of the yield pickup is attributable to the AMT status on the bond issue. The balance of the pickup is due to the callable nature and uncertain maturity date for the bond issue. Once again, in our opinion the yield to either maturity outcome is attractive versus other types of high quality bonds, but we also believe there is a high likelihood the bond will be redeemed in 2016 barring a substantial hike in interest rates.

AMT-subject municipals can be an excellent alternative for the investor that has the ability to utilize this type of security. A conversation with your tax advisor is always recommended prior to purchasing this type of municipal bond in order to determine the overall suitability.

CHAPTER 18

Size Matters

There are many nuances within the municipal bond market, and some of them are real head scratchers. We have all been taught in our professional careers that the more you buy of something, the better the chances are that a favorable price can be negotiated. A company like Walmart has often used its vast buying power to extract a lower price point from its suppliers. Logic tells me that if I purchase a million widgets I can get more favorable pricing than if I just buy ten. Therefore, logic would suggest if I buy $1,000,000 worth of municipal bonds I can get a better price than if I buy $10,000 worth. In reality, it is just the opposite.

Within the $3.8 trillion municipal bond market there are over 60,000 different issuers that have created over one million different issues of municipal bonds. Compare this to the 8,000 companies that make up the public U.S. equity market, and you can quickly realize the magnitude of the municipal market. Many of the issuers of municipal debt are small and come to market infrequently. The typical municipal bond issue will have a maturity schedule that encompasses 1 to 30 years and bonds will be scheduled to mature in most of those years. Let's say Pleasantville, USA plans to build a new high school for $30,000,000 and finance the school with a municipal bond issue. The debt will be paid back over a period of 30 years and the issue is structured with a debt schedule that pays back principal of $1,000,000 per year plus interest for the 30 year term. These payments are structured as individual maturities. The point is that prospective buyers will be faced with the potential to purchase a maximum of $1,000,000 in any given maturity. What if a potential buyer is a money manager that has $50 billion dollars under management? This buyer will typically need much larger piece sizes to include in their portfolios in order to make them strategically manageable. Therefore, this large money manager will seek out bigger size issues for their portfolios. The result is that in the high quality areas of the municipal market, the bigger the block, the higher the price you will have to pay. Of course there are always exceptions, such as during times of crisis or periods of illiquidity. But as a general rule, you will pay more for a $100,000 piece than a $25,000 block and pay more for a $1,000,000 piece than a $500,000 block and more for a $10,000,000 piece than a $1,000,000 block. When I say pay more, that is in terms of price, which results in a lower investment yield. We are often amused by the claims of the larger market participants indicating that their sheer size enables them to crowd out smaller buyers and dominate the larger block size issues, which in actuality trade more expensively.

When building out a high quality municipal portfolio, consider the size of the position that makes sense for your situation. A general guideline can be to maximize your individual positions to no more than 5% in any one issuer. This is done to minimize the credit risk associated with any one issuer that may experience financial hardship. If you are creating a total portfolio of $1,000,000, then purchase $50,000 pieces. This individual position size will help diversify the portfolio and allow the buyer to utilize the smaller, higher yielding piece sizes that are appropriate for the account.

CHAPTER 19

Trade Execution: Secondary Market

T he municipal bond market is an over-the-counter market. Transactions are executed manually. No exchange exists where an investor can go to access an individual municipal bond issue. There are exchange traded municipal bond ETFs and mutual funds, but these entities buy and sell the underlying holdings in their portfolios through direct contact with a buyer or seller. The market is just too diverse and fragmented to lend itself to an exchange trading platform. To paraphrase an old Smith Barney commercial, "We do it the old fashioned way." Accessing this market can be difficult for the lay investor. If an individual desires to position or purchase a municipal bond the first step may be to call their financial advisor or stock broker. The investor is shown an assortment of different bonds form that particular firm's inventory. The problem lies in that the firm may not have what the particular client needs or desires. The firm's representative may have very little real working knowledge of the municipal market. Even if the right security shows up on the firm's inventory at some point in time the investor and broker have to make contact in order to execute the trade, unless the client has authorized discretion to the broker. An individual may have to establish multiple relationships with different firms in order to find the appropriate mix of securities. Most investors are unwilling to go to this length and I can hardly blame them. I typically will deal with 40 to 50 broker-dealer firms in order to access inventory. This inventory is obviously much more diverse and broad in scope than what an individual firm may be able to provide. With this backdrop, let's explore some of the ways a municipal transaction can occur.

Ultimately there are owners of municipal bonds including individuals, insurance companies, mutual funds, hedge funds, etc. These owners transact with each other buying and selling through a network of broker dealer firms such as Merrill Lynch, Goldman Sachs, JP Morgan, etc. The owners need a broker dealer conduit to execute trades as there is no platform available to execute directly with one another. Let's say that the Safety Insurance Company has a portfolio of municipal bonds and determines it would be in their best interest to sell one of the positions. The portfolio manager at Safety will advertise he has a bond for sale and will typically utilize a financial based computer terminal such as Bloomberg to notify as many broker-dealer firms as he or she desires. These firms will enter bids at a specified time and the Bloomberg network will tabulate the results so our portfolio manager at Safety can evaluate the bids.

The bids will be ranked from high to low by dollar price. The portfolio manager at Safety will determine if selling at that price is agreeable and elect to either sell the bonds, not sell the bonds, or potentially decline to sell at the stated price but maybe set a somewhat higher price where he is willing to execute a trade. This decision will have to be made typically within an hour after the initial bid was due. The actual bids submitted will be from a variety of broker-dealer firms. Some of the firms will be bidding with the intention of placing the bonds in their inventory to re-market to clients after a price markup and this is called a "stock bid". Other broker dealers will be submitting bids on behalf of other ultimate buyers of municipals such as another insurance company and is called an "order bid" or a "bid versus order". This is where the over the counter part comes in to play. When a potential seller enters the market and advertises a block of bonds for the bid, hopefully one of the 50 broker-dealer firms we do business with will notice it is a type of bond I may care about. This knowledge of the client is paramount to putting buyer and seller together. For the types of bonds we prefer, most of our sales coverage knows what we look for and will show us the potential purchase candidate. This is how we typically trans-act trades and we will bid an item through a broker-dealer, then pay that dealer a very small transaction fee or commission but only if we are the high bidder and the seller agrees to sell. The commission is typically around 25 cents a bond or $250 for a block of $1 million. The broker-dealer involved in the trade is satisfied with the small commission because it is a riskless trans-action and they can look good to the seller of the bond and in-crease their market participation. Without my order, they may not even choose to bid the bond for their own inventory. At times there may be billions of dollars of municipals transacting every day with many different market participants. Through this malaise it all seems to come together and there really is a "method to the madness". Think of the process as an auto auction where various car dealers are bidding for cars, some to place on their lots for resale and some bidding for a client looking for a specific car to personally own.

What happens if the seller happens to be Merrill Lynch instead of our friend at Safety Insurance Company? At times a broker-dealer may want to sell a bond out of its own inventory. The bond may have been purchased a week ago, and they have been unable to resell it to a client at a price they feel is reasonable. The broker-dealer may choose to place his own bond "out for the bid" and seek a buyer. The difference is the broker-dealer does this anonymously through a specialized type of broker dealer called a broker's broker. This type of brokerage firm will advertise the Merrill Lynch bond to other broker-dealer firms on an electronic website and solicit bids. These firms have existed for many decades and have transacted billions of dollars of transactions over the years and you have probably never heard of any of them! J.J. Kenny, Chapdelaine, J.F. Hartfield, and R.W. Smith are just a few of these specialists present in the municipal market. In our example, if the bid they solicit is acceptable to Merrill Lynch, then Merrill will sell the bond directly to the broker's broker, who will then turn around and sell it to the ultimate buyer. The markup or commission is very small and typically approximates about 50 cents per bond or $500 per $1 million of bonds transacted. Neither the buyer nor the seller ever is told the ultimate identity of either party involved.

Notice all of this activity is executed in a competitive environment. This is not the case if an individual with limited knowledge of the market wishes to execute a trade. When individual investors wish to sell a municipal position, they will typically call their broker dealer where the account is held and ask to sell a position they own in the account. Unfortunately, this is not a competitive situation and the broker knows it. Very rarely would an individual investor ask multiple firms for a bid on a municipal bond. Would you ever sell a car to just one bidder without knowing what others in the market may pay?

CHAPTER 20

Accessing the Market for an Individual Investor

I n many of the previous chapters we have alluded to the different types of bonds available to the investing public and how the markets actually affect trades. If the endeavor of portfolio management seems too daunting of a task, investors may turn to a market professional for assistance. There are essentially three alternatives available to the general public for accessing the municipal bond market. These include: investing in a municipal bond mutual fund, purchasing individual bonds through a broker dealer firm, or hiring a fee based advisor to execute trades on your behalf. In this chapter, we will attempt to illustrate the pros and cons of each approach.

There are many municipal bond mutual funds available to the investor seeking to access the asset class. They vary widely in regards to quality, maturity, and costs. Our focus in this book has been on the high quality municipal market and we will limit this discussion to the investment grade mutual fund market. Generally speaking, mutual funds offer a professionally managed portfolio in exchange for a management fee. The fees vary widely among funds and range from an annual fee of 0.20% to as much as 4.00% of assets depending on the class of fund employed. Pay particular attention to any pre-penalty or early withdrawal fee. One suggestion would be to utilize a fund with a share class with the lowest fee possible. This may be available only through a direct investment with the mutual fund itself and not through a broker dealer firm. The advantages of a mutual fund are ease of valuation, liquidity, diversification, and professional management. For the investor with fewer available assets, this may be the only viable alternative in order to achieve an appropriate level of diversification in the portfolio. The downside of this type of investment is the inability to customize the portfolio for the individual investor and the nuances this investor may possess. The mutual fund invests more for the masses and strategies employed may not mirror what an individual investor in the fund is trying to accomplish. For instance, many of the topics we have discussed in this book may not be available through mutual fund investment. The investor can't control the distribution of capital gains or losses as this is at the discretion of the mutual fund manager. Another drawback is the mutual fund will typically invest with a constant average maturity as spelled out in the prospectus. Therefore, the portfolio can't be an effective buy and hold strategy if interest rates increase and the value of the fund drops. An investor in individual bond holdings has the advantage of riding out the storm and waiting for the maturity date to recoup any paper losses that may occur due to rising interest rates and falling market valuations. A third drawback is often an investor may have a much higher quality bias than the fund but has no control over that process and simply has to settle for the credit quality of the bonds selected for the fund. For example, while researching mutual funds in 2010, an analysis was performed on the holdings of the top 5 mutual funds ranked by assets under management. The analysis showed that 4 of the 5 funds held a 25% allocation in just two states, California and New York. This goes against what many investors feel is appropriate for those two states, especially since the financial crisis. The funds may also hold a position in other states where an individual investor may choose to avoid such as Illinois, Michigan, Nevada, Arizona, or even Puerto Rico. All of these states or territories have had a tougher time recovering from the effects of the financial crisis due to large drops in property values and the subsequent drop in state and local revenues. In my opinion, the benefits to owning individual bonds are significant. However, the advantages for the smaller investor with less than $500,000 make this type of municipal bond investment appropriate.

Direct investment in individual municipal bonds can also be executed through a broker dealer on a transactional basis. This type of arrangement is where an individual investor has a relationship with a sales person at a brokerage firm and contracts to buy on an individual bond basis for a transaction fee. These transactions can also be performed online at a discount brokerage firm. There is no ongoing fee as with the mutual fund company, only the onetime fee paid at purchase. The level of expertise can vary widely depending on the firm and individual chosen to assist in the execution of the transaction. A salesperson or stockbroker at a typical broker dealer firm may have less knowledge of the municipal market than a trained specialist in municipal bonds. The purchase made at a discount brokerage firm may leave all of the expertise to the buyer. Beyond the knowledge issues, the buyer is typically limited to only the inventory of that one individual brokerage firm. Depending on the firm, this inventory can be very limited. Once again, the ability to match an appropriate investment to the nuances of the client can be challenging. The fees charged for this type of market access can vary widely from firm to firm and even from salesperson to salesperson within the same firm. This lack of transparency can sometimes lead to an adversarial relationship between the client and the salesperson. The higher the fee that is charged, the lower the resulting yield to the investor becomes for the life of the transaction. A study conducted by the Wall Street Journal in 2014 determined the average fee charged to individual investors purchasing State of Washington General Obligation bonds from 2012 to 2013 was 1.73%. The complete article is attached in the Appendix. This level of fee can significantly lower the yield to the investor for the life of the bond.

The more significant drawback to investing through a broker dealer can be the lack of ongoing research available to the investor regarding the bonds held in the portfolio. Typically there is little if any research done after the sale is made even though the bond may have a maturity date of many years. The investment grade municipal market is extremely safe, but it is a different market than what existed prior to the financial crisis. It is imperative, in my opinion, to conduct ongoing credit surveillance on portfolio holdings. Unfortunately, at most brokerage firms, transactional business leaves the lion share of ongoing research up to the individual investor.

The final option available to the individual investor is to employ a fee based advisor to assist in the implementation of a municipal bond strategy. I would suggest choosing a manager that purchases individual bonds for the account versus purchasing mutual funds due to the many advantages individual bonds exhibit. There are many fee based advisors offering a wide variety of strategies for investing in municipal bonds. It is my recommendation to interview a number of potential firms to determine if the strategy fits the personal goals of the individual investor. Compare and contrast the firms' abilities and track record. Most registered investment advisors (RIAs) will be able to show a long term record relating to performance results from investing in municipal bonds. Beware of firms using hypothetical returns, and insist on actual performance of accounts under their management. The advantages of a fee based advisor can be professional bond management and a transparent investment process. A portfolio can typically be customized to mirror the objectives of the individual client. Most will offer ongoing research of the bonds purchased within the managed account. Generally, the only fees charged are based on the level or dollar amount of assets under management. A typical fee for this type of manager will range from .25% to .40% of the assets under management and is charged on an annual basis and paid quarterly.

For the investor with a level of assets that exceeds $1,000,000, I would recommend the fee based advisor due to the ability to customize the portfolio and offer ongoing credit research. The fees are similar to those charged by most mutual funds and all the advantages of owning individual holdings of bonds are available for the investor's benefit. The client-advisor relationship is not adversarial, and the best interests of the client can be put at the forefront of the relationship. It will take an amount of research on the part of the investor to find the manager that best fits the overall goals of the portfolio. Through this interview process, an investor will learn of the manager's experience investing in the asset class and the manager's performance record over the past years. Although this is not a guarantee of future results, you can at least gain an appreciation for how the manager has performed relative to a market benchmark. It is my suggestion to pay particular attention to how the manager performed in the year 2008, which in my opinion is a litmus test for managers of high quality bonds. If the performance results were excellent compared to peers in this time period, chances are you have found a manager that can perform in times of stress.

CHAPTER 21

Portfolio Construction

Now that we have managed to navigate through many of the various high quality sectors of municipal bonds that possess above market yield characteristics, we need to build out a portfolio that will mirror our objectives. These objectives can be diverse in nature. The portfolio may be intended for an individual, insurance company, corporation, or other investor. Each entity may have varying needs for the portfolio including liquidity, asset liability management, income, principal preservation, etc. Tax treatment on income may differ depending on marginal tax bracket, state of residency, or AMT (Alternative Minimum Tax) status. All of these factors have implications for how the portfolio will be created. We will concentrate our discussion of building a portfolio for an individual investor.

It is my belief that an individual investor seeking safety of principal, income, and low price volatility within a municipal bond portfolio is best suited with an intermediate maturity strategy. The yields available will typically be higher than a short term maturity strategy and yet not have the price volatility of a longer maturity strategy. Finding the balance of yield and price stability is a tricky proposition. Historically speaking, over the past 15 years the returns from an intermediate versus long term maturity strategy equates to approximately 50 basis points in performance on an annualized basis in favor of the longer term strategy (Source: Barclays Municipal Bond Indices as of (12/31/2013). I feel this is not sufficient to justify the increased price volatility of the longer term portfolio. An intermediate portfolio will have bonds that typically range in maturity from one to fifteen years and have an average maturity of five to seven years. It is important to ladder all of the potential outcomes from a maturity perspective. For instance if you purchase callable bonds, ladder the portfolio to both the call date and final maturity date. Use many of the structures outlined in this commentary to potentially maximize your yield at purchase date.

Diversification is the key to avoiding potential pitfalls within the municipal market. A broad dispersion of issuers is one way to minimize the impact of a potential deterioration of credit. In a high quality portfolio, maximize any one holding to no more than 5% of the portfolio value. Diversify across issuer type such as general obligation and revenue bonds. Diversify geographically and avoid the more at risk states from an economic point of view. Taxation at the state level is a component of portfolio management but should not be the driving force behind geographic security selection. With the types of bonds outlined in this commentary, the yield pickup is substantially greater than the offset of having to pay state income tax on out of state bond income. Furthermore, diversify the portfolio revenue stream by utilizing many types of bonds, such as water and sewer, sales tax, utility tax, university, and excise tax bonds. Purchase bonds that have a high degree of essentiality for the project that is being financed. Invest with the mindset that if the economy turns south for a municipality what will be more important, the water and sewer plant or the city owned golf course? Just use a common business practice approach and view the investment as if you are truly lending the municipality funds in a private transaction. It is our belief that following these simple guidelines will go a long way towards protecting your investment and reaping all the benefits the asset class has to offer.

CHAPTER 22

Summary

I hope you have enjoyed this review of the municipal market and now have an appreciation for some of the nuances that can be present. The search for higher yields does not have to translate to investing in municipal bond strategies that utilize lower quality or longer maturity bonds. Those strategies are not appropriate for the investor who is investing in municipals in order to earn a stable source of income while preserving capital. There are many different structures of bonds in the marketplace that will offer higher investment yields. If the investor purchases relatively short-term bonds from a maturity perspective, certain structures offering higher yields can be acquired and held to maturity. This helps negate the market risk from rising interest rates. The overall strategy is to buy a cheaper asset and bleed that asset for the extra yield produced for as long as possible. If you consistently purchase bonds with higher than market yields it is my belief you should outperform the market over time. At times the sectors will also overlap. For instance, a callable bond with a sinking fund is quite common. Therefore, it takes the ability to analyze that combination of structures from all the different perspectives. Just remember that diversification is your best friend.

Remember, no matter how attractive an individual position appears to be, limit the exposure to no more than 5% of the investment portfolio. Utilize many different sectors of the market and concentrate on bonds with a high degree of essentiality. Regardless of the state of the economy, residents of a community will still need to turn on the water and lights. Diversify geographically first at the state level then at a regional and local level to avoid natural disaster and political risk. Finally, ladder all the potential maturity dates to reduce the exposure to changes in interest rates. Ladder even if the overall maturity profile is relatively short term. I feel by structuring the account with bonds coming due in each year or range of years, you will help insulate the portfolio from interest rate risk and unexpected emergency withdrawals. Utilizing these guidelines should enable the investor to create a portfolio that can potentially preserve capital while enjoying a stream of tax exempt interest for years to come. You have worked hard to accumulate these assets and it is our belief you should be able to enjoy the fruits of your efforts.

APPENDIX

As appeared in the *Wall Street Journal*, March 10, 2014

BY MATT WIRZ

Muni Bond Costs Hit Investors in Wallet

I nvestors who put cash into municipal bonds—a widely popular strategy for those seeking safe, tax-free bets—are paying about twice as much in trading commissions as they would for corporate bonds, according to a study for The Wall Street Journal.

Regulators largely bypassed municipal debt as they transformed much of Wall Street over the past 20 years, but are studying it more closely now.

Individuals are the biggest participants in the $3.7 trillion industry, which provides funding for states, cities, hospitals and school districts across the country.

A study of 53,000 municipal and corporate bonds by S&P Dow Jones Indices for The Journal shows how much more investors are trading for the municipal assets.

Individual investors trading $100,000 in bonds of a municipality, such as Washington State, in December paid brokers an average "spread" of 1.73%, or $1,730. That compares with 0.87%, or $870, paid on a comparable corporate bond, such as one issued by General Electric Capital Corp., the data show.

Brokers of stocks and corporate bonds must disclose market pricing and give individuals "best execution" on trades, ensuring they receive the best prices possible. In the municipal-bond industry, those protections are absent, allowing brokers to pocket higher spreads by buying the bonds low and selling them high.

Individual investors, especially retirees, have long been attracted to municipal debt as a relatively safe investment whose interest payments aren't taxed. They own 45% of all municipal bonds directly and another 28% through mutual funds, amounting to a combined $2.7 trillion, according to data from the Federal Reserve.

The market is supervised by several regulators and structured differently than the stock and corporate-debt markets, and regulation of muni-bond trading has been slow to evolve.

"I think we can do more here for retail investors," said Michael Piwowar, one of five commissioners on the Securities and Exchange Commission, in an interview. "We spend an awful lot of time on the equities side of the market where spreads are counted in pennies—and in the "muni" market, spreads are counted in dollars."

Brokerages say that municipal bonds cost more to trade because they change hands far less frequently and in smaller amounts than do other securities. They have warned that regulatory changes could hurt activity in the municipal market.

The SEC held hearings on the issue in 2010 and 2011 and proposed changes in a 2012 report, but they haven't been implemented.

Investors bought and sold $183 billion of municipal bonds last year in trades of $100,000 or less, in line with recent years, according to data from the Municipal Securities Rulemaking Board.

One of those investors was Jack Leonard, a 67-year-old resident of Ipswich, Mass., who on July 23 sold bonds promising a 5% annual interest payment from his home state in two lots of $100,000 each.

The broker buying the bonds told Mr. Leonard the best price he could get was about $1,030 per bond, or $206,000.

The following day, a broker sold the same amount of 5% bonds to investors for $1,060 a bond, or $212,000, according to an online history of trading prices maintained by the MSRB. The difference of $6,000 in the two transactions is equal to 3% of the bonds' value.

It wasn't possible to verify that both trades involved Mr. Leonard's bonds from the MSRB database, which doesn't identify trade participants. But in July, MSRB records show brokers collectively sold $1 million in Massachusetts bonds to investors at a 3% average markup from the prices they paid for them, amounting to $30,000 in profits.

"That's a lot of money, and the real question is: Why are they allowed to do it?" said Mr. Leonard.

The SEC oversees the MSRB, which sets rules for the industry, and the Financial Industry Regulatory Authority, which enforces them. Oversight coordination has been poor at times because the market is supervised by three regulators rather than one and the issue has had a low priority in Washington, said Hester Peirce, a former SEC staff attorney who is now a research fellow at George Mason University in Arlington, Va. "I think it's going to be under more scrutiny" going forward, she said, referring to Mr. Piwowar's push and recent proposals by the MSRB.

MSRB Executive Director Lynnette Kelly said the board "is working closely with the SEC to address market structure issues in a realistic time frame." John Nester, a spokesman for the SEC, said his group and others "work cooperatively on issues affecting the municipal securities market." Staff from Finra and the MSRB meet frequently "to ensure and sustain this collaborative approach," a Finra spokesman said.

Proposed changes face opposition from brokers, which fund both the MSRB and Finra. Firms such as Charles Schwab & Co. and Wells Fargo Advisors LLC have lobbied against some changes.

"The devil is always in the details when it comes to new regulations, but we commend the MSRB for bringing this issue forward and urge them to continue this important effort," said Jeff Brown, senior vice president of legislative and regulatory affairs at Schwab. Wells Fargo declined to comment.

Meanwhile, the lack of pricing information gives mom-and-pop investors little leverage to negotiate.

"I don't know what the market is, because they won't show me," said Mike Becker, a retired options trader. The 70-year-old Boca Raton, Fla., resident said he has grown frustrated trying to get his broker at the Merrill Lynch unit of Bank of America Corp. to tell him the best bid being offered for the Florida state bonds he wants to sell and has petitioned the SEC to pass rules giving "the public a fairer shake."

"We have policies and procedures in place that adhere to MSRB guidelines as they pertain to fair pricing," a Merrill spokeswoman said.

The MSRB proposed a municipal-bond best-execution rule last week that it hopes to enact this year or next and is working on a digital pricing platform, a person familiar with the matter said.

MSRB Chairman Dan Heimowitz, a banker at RBC Capital Markets Corp., said he is working to balance necessary changes against the risk that a rushed overhaul could spur brokers to quit the market, making it harder for individuals to trade. "That is why we go slowly and methodically, but we haven't given up on this by any means," he said.

Mr. Piwowar, a former economist who studied trading costs in corporate and municipal bonds, is pushing for fixes he hopes the SEC can enact this year, like requiring brokers to give clients more price information ahead of potential trades. He said stock and corporate-bond brokers also complained that similar reforms would stifle trading when it was imposed on their markets, "but in fact, all the evidence suggests the opposite."

Peter Coffin, a municipal-bond manager for wealthy individuals at Boston-based Breckenridge Capital Advisors, said it is about time the muni market got an overhaul. "You think of how the retail industry has gone from the local grocery store to Walmart to Amazon," he said. By contrast, he said, "In municipal bonds, we're still shopping at the local grocery store."

DISCLOSURE STATEMENT

Please read these disclosures carefully before you invest. Investing in the bond market involves risk and may not be suitable for all investors. Information presented herein is subject to change without notice and should not be considered as a solicitation to buy or sell any security. For a full list of all recommendations made by Crawford during the last year, please contact Casey Krimmel at the information below.

The holdings identified throughout the [presentation] were selected to help illustrate the investment strategy described in each of the case studies. Performance was not a criteria used in the selection process. Information contained herein should not be construed as personalized investment advice. Not every client account will have these exact characteristics. The actual characteristics with respect to any particular client account will vary based on a number of factors including but not limited to: (i) the size of the account; (ii) investment restrictions applicable to the account, if any; and (iii) market conditions at the time of investment. Different types of investments involve varying degrees of risk, and there can be no assurance that any specific investment will be profitable. Crawford reserves the right to modify its current investment strategies and techniques based on changing market dynamics or client needs. It should not be assumed that any of the securities, holdings or sectors discussed were or will prove to be profitable, or that the investment recommendations or decisions we make in the future will be profitable. Additionally, there is no assurance that any holdings discussed are or will remain in an account's portfolio at the time the investor receive this [report] or that securities sold have not been repurchased. Crawford reserves the right to modify its current investment strategies and techniques based on changing market dynamics or client needs. The securities discussed may not represent an account's entire portfolio and in the aggregate may represent only a small percentage of an account's portfolio holdings.

Crawford utilizes best efforts that content provided is compiled or derived from sources believed to be reliable and accurate, but makes no representation or warranties as to the accuracy, completeness or timeliness of the information, text, graphics or other items contained in this [presentation]. Crawford expressly disclaims all liability for errors or omissions in, or the misuse or misinterpretation of, any information contained in this presentation.

Crawford Investment Counsel is an independent registered investment advisor with the U.S. Securities and Exchange Commission. Registration does not imply a certain level of skill or training. More information about Crawford, including its investment strategies, objectives and fees can be found in its Form ADV Part 2, which is available, without charge, upon request. The Crawford Form ADV Part 2 also contains information regarding its business practices and the backgrounds of its key personnel. Past Performance is not necessarily indicative of future results and the value of investments and the income they generate can fluctuate. CRA-14-14

CRAWFORD INVESTMENT COUNSEL
600 Galleria Parkway, Suite 1650
Atlanta, GA 30339 770-859-0045
www.crawfordinvestment.com